DO YOURSELF A FAVOR
Tips and Quips on the Writing Life

By Michelle L. Levigne

Michelle L. Levigne

Mt Zion Ridge Press
295 Gum Springs Rd, NW
Georgetown, TN 37366

www.MtZionRidgePress.com

Copyright © 2018 by Michelle L. Levigne
ISBN 13: 978-1-949564-30-3

Published in the United States of America
Publication Date: March 15, 2019

Editor-In-Chief: Michelle Levigne
Executive Editor: Tamera Lynn Kraft

Cover Art Copyright by Mt Zion Ridge Press © 2019
Images taken from www.Pixabay.com:
typewriter-vintage-write-letters-1170657/
letters-numbers-blocks-alphabet-691842/
pencil-sharpener-notebook-paper-918449/

All rights reserved. No portion of this book may be reproduced or transmitted in any form or by any electronic or mechanical means, including photocopying, recording or by any information retrieval and storage system without permission of the publisher.

Ebooks, audiobooks, and print books are *not* transferrable, either in whole or in part. As the purchaser or otherwise *lawful* recipient of this book, you have the right to enjoy the novel on your own computer or other device. Further distribution, copying, sharing, gifting or uploading is illegal and violates United States Copyright laws.

Pirating of books is illegal. Criminal Copyright Infringement, *including* infringement without monetary gain, may be investigated by the Federal Bureau of Investigation and is punishable by up to five years in federal prison and a fine of up to $250,000.

Names, characters and incidents depicted in this book are products of the author's imagination, or are used in a fictitious situation. Any resemblances to actual events, locations, organizations, incidents or persons – living or dead – are coincidental and beyond the intent of the author.

Do Yourself a Favor: Tips and Quips on the Writing Life

TABLE OF CONTENTS

PREFACE	1
AUTHORS' 10 COMMANDMENTS	2
INTRODUCTION/EXPLANATION/DISCLAIMER/WHATEVER	3

THE PREPARATION PHASE:

WRITING = COOKING	9
PUBLISHING IS WAR	13
SOMETHING TO SAY -- BUT *SHOULD* YOU?	15
WHOSE RULES?	
MASTER THE RULES BEFORE YOU BREAK THEM	17
PLOTTERS VS. PANTSERS	20
DECISIONS BEFORE YOU GET STARTED	23
HUMILIATING CONFESSION TIME	29
THAT IDEA STORE	31
THE PERILS AND PITFALLS AND PLUSSES OF WRITING	
-- OR THINKING OF WRITING -- A SERIES	33
ARE YOU READY?	37

TOOLS, EDUCATION, AND SUPPORT:

WHO ARE YOU TALKING TO?	41
READ FOR YOUR CAREER	43
HOW TO LOSE WRITING CONTESTS	44
PRACTICE WHAT YOU PREACH WHILE YOU'RE PREACHING	47
WRITING CONFERENCES -- GO!	49
EVERYBODY NEEDS FRIENDS	52
THE RIGHT WORD VS. THE ALMOST-RIGHT WORD	59
WORDS, WORDS, WORDS	60
PUNCTUATION CRIMES	67
SENTENCE STRUCTURE RANT	71
REALMIES RULE!	73
THERE'S RICH, AND THEN THERE ARE RICHES	76

THE WRITING PHASE:

YOU'RE THE DIRECTOR	79
SHOW -- DON'T TELL -- THROUGH SCREENWRITING	81
FILLING IN THE WHITE SPACES	83
JALAPENOS = BACKSTORY	86

CONSISTENCY IS SURVIVAL	87
USE YOUR OWN VOCAB, PLEASE?	89
DO YOU HOP?	91
HOW DID HE KNOW THAT?	93
ARE YOU AN OBJECT OR A SUBJECT?	96
"BLEAH," "MEH," OR "YEAH!" ?	97
FAIR USE -- EMPHASIS ON *FAIR*	99
BUTTON HOLES, NOT THE WHOLE DRESS	102
GET TO THE END!	104
NEVER THROW OUT ANYTHING	106
GET YOURSELF SOME FRESH EYES	108
REVISIONS: YES, YOU *MUST*	110
EVEN WHEN IT STOPS BEING FUN?	112

THE SELLING PHASE:

THE UGLY TRUTH -- PROMOTION	117
PR, MARKETING, AND EDUCATION	119
EDITORS AND AGENTS	124
THE QUEST FOR COVER ART	131
IN CONCLUSION	133

About the Author

PREFACE

Like the Pirates' Code, many alleged "rules" of writing are more like guidelines...

But don't believe anyone who insists there are NO rules for writing. There are rules: the mechanics. The craft, as opposed to the art. They are equivalent to the tools for sculpting clay or stone, or spinning and dyeing thread for weaving, or learning to play scales, read music, and keep your instrument in tune when creating music. The rest -- the "art" portion -- is flexible and adapts to what works best for YOU the writer. The technique for playing the instrument, the point of view and voice for the story, the genre you write in, the images you create from stone and clay, the pattern of the cloth you weave, and the colors you choose to use.

When you understand the why of the rules, then you can bend or break them.

- ✓ So *Do Yourself A Favor* and learn what's hard-and-fast, and what is flexible. It'll save you pain and effort and wasted time in the long run.

This collection of advice started as blog postings (read: semi-rants) while editing people who had something to say, but didn't take the time to figure out *how* to say it. Basically, whenever I ran into something noteworthy (embarrassing, frustrating, amusing, revelatory) in my own writing journey, or things I encountered too often in editing, I blogged about them. Not from ego and "Hey, look at what a genius I am!" (at least, I hope not) but in the belief that the things that frustrated or fascinated me would be helpful to others. Along with those blog posts, revised because of timeliness or to cover a broader subject, or to fit in new discoveries along the way, I offer bits of advice about topics that other authors have found worthy of discussion. Or argument. Or mockery. Or complaint. Or wailing. Or amusement of the I'm-losing-my-mind variety.

This is sort of a bits-and-pieces offering, touching on a LOT of different areas, things that some newer writers might not have heard about or run into yet. If you're looking for in-depth treatises on specific subjects, I strongly recommend people like James Scott Bell, Steven James, Brandilyn Collins, Orson Scott Card, Anne Lamott, and all the titles in the Writers Digest Fiction Writers series. This is a sampler of things I believe anyone who says they're serious about writing should keep in mind. Things I don't want to see if you submit your book to me as your editor or publisher. Just saying ...

Snark warning!

AUTHORS' 10 COMMANDMENTS

By Julie Gwinn
Agent with the Seymour Agency
Used with permission

#10 Thou Shall Write What You Know. #ownvoices is trending now for a reason. If you live in Australia, write about Australia. If you are in the military, write military fiction. #amwriting

#9 Thou Shall Do Research. Know basic word counts for books, know your genre or subgenre, look at submission guidelines before sending the email.

#8 Thou Shall Read What You Write. If you write YA, read YA. If you write romantic suspense, read romantic suspense. It helps you pick up nuances within the genre

#7 Thou Shall Ask Others To Read Your Writing. A crit partner, beta readers, writers group, awards committee...someone other than a spouse

#6 Thou Shall Post, Blog, Tweet, Heart, comment, video on social media to tell others about your book.

#5 Thou Shall Never Give Up. Rejection is part of publishing, is part of life. If you have characters, a story that has to come out, keep writing, keep submitting, keep learning and trying.

#4 Thou Shall Keep Your Motivation For Writing In-Check And Have Clear Goals. Do you write to change lives or to win awards? Do you write to tell a story or to make an Amazon list? #amwriting

#3 Thou Shall NOT Compare Yourself, Your Sales, Your Work, Your Reviews To Other Authors. There are so many variables in publishing, some out of your control. Comparing yourself to others is destructive.

#2: Thou Shall Continue To Learn And Grow As A Writer. Attend conferences, read books on writing, try different genres, try different tropes.

#1 Thou Shall Find Time Every Day To Write. No excuses.

INTRODUCTION/EXPLANATION/DISCLAIMER/WHATEVER

So, what gives me the authority to offer you some advice, to help you avoid falling into some of the pits and traps or ramming your head against some big, unfriendly walls on the way to publication?

I'm speaking to you as someone who has been making a living as a freelance editor for ten-plus years, has made the shift to small press publisher, and has (or had) more than 100 titles in print and e-book. (Warning: the more prolific you are, the bigger your chances of having some of your books orphaned at one time or another. This is an unstable world you've entered, the realm called Publication.)

I must be doing *something* right!

Or not.

The jury is still out. Like, out of this universe sometimes ...

See, here's the funny thing about the writing life:

Other than the mechanics, as mentioned earlier, the hard science of language and those funny marks on the page or screen, a lot of what makes up fiction writing or poetry writing or screenwriting or what have you (the "fun" writing, I'm not talking about textbooks and how-to manuals or cookbooks, although some people think cooking does qualify as fun) -- a lot of this is *flexible*.

As in, there are no real hard-and-fast rules. Not everywhere. Not all the time.

(Warning: I'm going to repeat myself a lot, because there is some harmful teaching out there to deprogram or defuse, take your pick. Harmful teaching from people who insist <u>their way</u> is the <u>only way to write</u>, as well as harmful teaching from well-meaning folks who also believe what works for them is the only way. The only difference is they're not so stiff-necked and nasty and condemning as the ones who promise you will <u>never be published</u> if you don't do it <u>their way</u>.)

This fun tidbit feeds into the belief going around that all creative writers are kinda nuts (because yeah, a few are, and then there are the ones who use the voices in their heads as an excuse to become alcoholics or drug addicts). Memorize this, because it'll save you some fried brain circuits and ulcers: *Once you learn the rules, you earn the right to break them as you see fit, to suit the needs of the story you're telling.* Because once you understand the rules, how they work, why they're there, then you know *how* to break them without upsetting the balance of the universe and speeding up the downward plunge into illiteracy and anarchy of the entire Human race.

Of course, that could be taken as a matter of opinion and not hard fact. I'm just passing on what I've learned, from my observations and experience, and not engraving it in stone. If you disagree with me, I'm not going to argue, so return the favor, okay?

- ✓ So *Do Yourself A Favor* as early in your writing journey as you can: Learn the rules, master them, learn *why* they are there (that's more important than memorizing and slavishly following them, because there are always exceptions), and then you'll know when and where and why and how to break those rules, and be justified in doing so.

(Because someone out there is going to demand you justify what you did, sometimes with a threat of dueling pistols at dawn and twenty paces, or a severe lashing with wet noodles.)

As someone who has dealt with the confusing and sometimes painful excuses for books that some people want to publish, I know there are some hard and fast rules that must never, on pain of death or the opening of the Abyss, be broken. I'll let you know when we get to those rules. Trust me. The snark factor will go up exponentially when we get to certain areas where people who don't know the difference between *affect* and *effect*, or *insure, assure,* and *ensure*, or *their, there,* and *they're* think they've produced a book. People who think that just vomiting their thoughts into the computer is all they have to do, meaning they have no responsibility to make it readable or at least give readers a fighting chance to understand what they've said. People who think that five handwritten pages qualifies as a book (umm, no, that's a brochure, at best). People who don't pay attention to the worlds and characters they create, so the hair color or eye color or make of car or name of their main character changes multiple times through the book. Then they get upset when people say their story is confusing. The same people who cry like a toddler with dirty diapers and try to make you the villain in the piece when you point out their mistakes.

As I said earlier, a lot of what some people consider rules are more like guidelines, because writing *is* art. Yes, even genre fiction.

Don't get me started on people who consider themselves writers of "literature," and look down their long, arrogant noses at people who write genre fiction. I'm serious. Don't get me started. Along the lines of Dr. Banner advising the reporter, McGee, not to make him angry. I've trimmed out a lot of snark as it is from this final draft of the book. (Many thanks and kudos to *Bettie Boswell* and *Kat Vinson* for their input and beta-reading skills!)

Other than the mechanics of grammar, spelling, and punctuation, and all their awful, headache-inducing permutations, most of writing is covered under the heading of "whatever works for YOU."

- ✓ *Do Yourself A Favor*: remember that, okay?

It'll save you some headaches and angst, and help you walk away from arguments with people who try to fit you into their cramped little boxes of what a writer should do and think and be. Or worse, the people with cookie cutters, who want to cut away all the "dough" of your creativity and the unique way your mind works. They try their hardest to make everyone's books look and feel and sound and smell and taste the same, but a dessert buffet with only one kind of cookie is boring, don't you think? They're trying to make you produce their favorite cookie, when you're not planning on making cookies at all!

Remember: find and then use the methods that work for you, and don't let anyone tell you you're wrong. At the same time, keep learning and experimenting. Just because you've found something that works for you *right now*, that doesn't mean you can't change and grow -- you've found what works *now*, but you might find something even better a few years from now.

- ✓ *Do Yourself A Favor*: throw out (or dodge) those cookie cutters aimed at your mind and creativity.

Remember: Just because a method works for YOU, don't you dare impose it on someone else and insist that they can't do it any other way.

Remember this, too: If you don't agree with me (except where it comes to mechanics), feel free to ignore me. I'm just passing on what I've learned, what I've observed, what I've heard other writers gripe about and laugh about (with a heavy dose of, "Can you *believe* this wacko?"). Use what works for you and leave the rest behind for someone else to pick up and adapt for their own needs.

- ✓ *Do Yourself A Favor*: write it down somewhere -- tattooed inside your eyelids? -- so you won't forget and get yourself tangled into knots when something I say contradicts what someone else (smarter, more talented, more popular, nicer -- take your pick) says.

Relax! Enjoy the trip! All the writing rules and tips and advice and guidelines are basically a gargantuan smorgasbord. It's *your* responsibility to figure out what will nourish you and what will give you hives, or have you making a panicky dash to the restrooms.

Disclaimer statement: Because what I'm sharing is what I've learned and observed, and because art is so flexible and personalized, I hereby grant you permission to laugh in the face of anyone who insists there is only one way: **their way**. (I can't give you permission to drop a house on them, because that could make me liable for broken bones, or at least their missing ruby slippers.) *Everybody* has a different approach. You've heard the Pantsers Vs. Plotters debate? Well, joy ... I'm a plontser. And sometimes I'm more a plantser, depending on how organized I get, or how much I need to plan out before I write.

I hereby give you permission to break some of what other people have vehemently declared are hard-and-fast rules, but *only* when you have a good reason to do so. And no, I'm not going to judge if your reason is good or not. So don't ask! (How can I write my own masterpieces if I'm checking everybody else's books all the time?)

More than anything else: HAVE FUN!!

That book you're writing is your private mental and emotional and imaginary PLAYGROUND, remember?

THE PREPARATION PHASE:

WRITING = COOKING

You wouldn't call yourself a chef just because you could fry an egg, would you?

Yet so many people out there think it's easy to be a writer, and they jump into writing a book without any preparation. They think because they passed high school English class (by the skin of their teeth, maybe -- because their teachers didn't want to deal with them any longer), that qualifies them. They think because they can speak the English language, then they can write.

Side note: according to what I hear all around me in the stores, on the bus, at the ball park, NO, most people can't speak English. They murderize it!

Most of my income is earned by freelance editing, receiving assignments from several publishing companies. One is a self-publishing company. The books go through an assessment process to determines how much editing they need. The authors pick the level or intensity of editing they want, and then the book is passed on to the stable of editors. (*Moi.*)

Some just need a mechanical edit: grammar, spelling and punctuation need to be checked and fixed.

Some need a line edit: this is a mechanical edit, plus more attention is paid to things like logical flow or clarity of thought, consistency in viewpoint, verb tense, and other details. For instance: "On page 5, you said her only child was named Fred. Here you say she has twin daughters. Please explain and fix." Or: "2 paragraphs ago, they were driving, now they're walking. When/where did they park the car and get out?" Or, "They sat down in the restaurant and the first thing the waiter did was bring them the bill. Shouldn't they order and eat before they pay?" (Actual questions I had to ask clients!)

Some need a developmental edit: basically, dissecting every single sentence, untangling mangled syntax, making suggestions for missing words, asking what the author was trying to say, correcting misquotes, fixing mistakes in references to real people and events or simple facts, and making suggestions for the author to expand. For instance: "On page 20, you promise you will give a list of the 10 characteristics of #####. On page 60 you made the same promise, and on page 95. We are on the last page, and you still haven't given that list." Or, "In the Table of Contents, you list ten chapters. None of the chapter titles in the text match the chapter titles in the Table of Contents. You have fourteen chapters. Please fix." Yeah. That bad. And worse.

Side note: I am tired of editing books based on the rewritten history learned from Saturday morning cartoons or Disney films or -- I am dismayed to admit -- the adapted theology of VeggieTales. No, the people of Jericho did not drop slushies on the Israelites as they marched around the walls. No, Pocahontas did not marry

John Smith, she married John Rolfe. The history of the world according to Walt Disney is just as false as the history of the world according to Mel Brooks!

Where was I?

Basically, a lot of people think they have something important -- nay, not important, but vital to the continued existence of the Human race -- that they must impart. However, they apparently don't find it equally as vital to take the time to either learn *how* to say it, or to make sure they said it correctly. To clarify: how to say it so that any average reader who picks up their book will be able to read it and come to the same conclusions the author holds dear. From some of the mangled messes I've been handed to turn into coherent English, chances are good these "authors" never opened a book in their lives, and don't know detail one about how books are organized -- yet they say they've written a book.

(An editing client sent me twelve files by email, after I told him [and he agreed to do so] to send his book as one file, in Times New Roman 12pt font, with one-inch margins. This is known as standard submission format. I thought the twelve files were twelve chapters, but they turned out to be JPG files. Not text files of any kind. [My mistake, expecting him to know a book should be in a text file?] He had scanned the typed pages of his "book" -- one file for each *page*. Twelve sheets of paper, with maybe fifty words on each page. There was no clue to the order of the pages. No page numbers. No table of contents. No chapter numbers or titles. He thought that was a book? Ummm ... No.)

People who think they have "natural talent" and don't need training are like a man who thinks he is a chef and knows all about food because he likes to eat. He doesn't know the difference between salt and sugar, between a frying pan and an angel food cake pan, and is offended when you ask him what recipe he's going to use.

Recipe? I don't need no stinkin' recipe!

What's really sad is that a lot of these people would never think to do auto repairs or apply for a job that they couldn't perform without some training. Yet they neglect the slightest bit of preparation before they sit down to write a book. They think if they have an idea and some way of recording it, then they are automatically writers.

Because writing is easy, don't you know?

Well, yeah, writing IS easy.

If you don't pay attention to what you're saying or where you're going.

If you don't have any real planned destination for this thought trail you're blazing.

If you don't listen to yourself/read what you've just written.

If you don't ask anyone else to read it and apply what you're teaching and tell you if they understand what you're trying to say.

If you only want to say you've *written* a book, and you never take the next step of trying to *sell* the book and get it into the hands of readers.

Honestly, I edited a book that I swear someone dictated into their computer, because there was no punctuation. The only capital letter was the first one at the top of the page. Each alleged "chapter" was a new recording file. The author probably had a conniption when the person doing the assessment said, "There's no punctuation, there's no capitalization, it's full of mis-spelled words, there's no clarity of thought because there is no punctuation, so this needs a developmental edit." Which of course costs three times as much as the basic edit.

More on this later.

- ✓ *Do Yourself a Favor*: Your first rule of survival as a writer who will be read someday is to …

… wait for it …

READ your book before you send it out. Even if you're just sending it to someone to read and tell you what they think, you *must* read it first. If only to catch the really stupid mistakes. Like constantly writing "manger" when you mean "manager," and other silly, embarrassing, just-how-dang-lazy-ARE-you glitches.

Because writing is only easy when you don't care.

Which doesn't make sense, because why would you spend the time writing your thoughts down if you didn't care?

Why waste the time and the thought and the energy, if you're not going to make every effort to be as clear and coherent as possible?

More important: What gives you the right to waste the time of other people, and force them to untangle your knotted thoughts and mangled syntax and atrocious spelling? (Snark warning, remember?)

So don't go into the kitchen and set out to cook a gourmet feast when you can barely figure out how to keep the pot from boiling over, okay? Just because Grandpa said you were a gourmet cook, that doesn't mean you are.

In fact, when it comes to proofreading and getting helpful critiques for your book -- which you will always need, even after you have a couple published titles under your belt -- never, ever, no matter how desperate you are, depend on your *relatives* to do that. Either they're going to be nasty and sabotage you right and left, or they're going to be "helpful" and ignore all the mistakes, because they don't want to hurt your itty bitty tender feelings. If they're just as helpless in basic grammar, spelling and punctuation as you are, they can have good intentions, but will just make things worse. And for heaven's sake, never, ever, on pain of public humiliation, wait until you're at a book signing before you hand your newly published book to your relatives and friends. If you must ask for their input, do it before you send the manuscript to the publisher.

Why? If you ask for their help before the book is printed, once they get their hands on the finished copy they won't dare open their mouths and point out the mistakes that <u>they didn't catch</u>. Simple survival skills.

- ✓ *Do Yourself A Favor*: get help from people who *know* what they're doing! That means don't ask your relatives unless they have English degrees, or they work in publishing or advertising or something where they actually think about the words they use all day.

In other words: Go into the kitchen with someone who knows the tools and the ingredients and how to use the cookbook. (You are following the metaphors and similes I'm using, right?) Watch him or her work. Ask questions. Listen when he or she talks about silly mistakes others have made. Pay attention to stories of glorious surprises that resulted from experiments *after* someone mastered those tools and ingredients. As you learn the tools and rules and combinations, what to do and not do, then you can experiment.

Sometimes you have to throw out what didn't turn out as you intended.

Sometimes you have to bury it.

The important thing is to learn and to grow and to gain skill.

Even more important -- have fun! Work your way up to the complex stuff while you're enjoying yourself. Lay a foundation for your imagination, and have a big dream as your goal.

When you know what you're doing, then you can put your visions into concrete form. Say you want to make a wedding cake with all sorts of figures made of marzipan and spun sugar, twenty layers, with ganache and fondant, and side cakes connected to it with sugar bridges, and pillars separating the fifteenth and sixteenth layers so you can insert a little fountain with colored lights and flowers. If you've never done anything more complicated than brownies that were half-cinder in your Easy-Bake Oven ... maybe you should start with cupcakes.

Know what I mean?

PUBLISHING IS WAR

When you join the military, do they send you onto the battlefield with spitballs instead of guns?

So why do people who decide to be writers slap words onto the page and never take the time to polish, proofread, fix grammar, spelling, punctuation, sentence structure, formatting, etc., before they send those words to a publisher?

Yes, I know what you're about to say: **Fixing those piddling little details are what editors are for.**

Umm… No! A traditional publisher will read the first paragraph of such a sloppy "masterpiece" (monsterpiece!) and reject it immediately. No publisher has the time and budget to make your book readable.

That is *your* job.

Before you submit.

If it's going to take hours of drudgery just fixing the things you should have caught with the spell check in your word processing software, no publisher worth her salt is going to buy the book. Time is money, after all.

As a side note: I'm a regular judge for a writing contest where the prize is a publishing package. One of the criteria for picking entries worth a second read is how much editing has to be done to make those entries publishable. I'm not going to inflict mental anguish and frustration that I wouldn't want to endure on another editor. That's just plain inconsiderate and cruel.

The only publishers who accept manuscripts full of grammar, spelling, punctuation and formatting mistakes **charge you** to fix them. Remember, I make my living as a freelance editor for people who self-publish, or publishers who contract to publish people's books *for them*. Books that traditional publishers won't touch because they're aimed at audiences too small to be profitable, or they are incoherent messes. Spitballs instead of rifles.

Remember that editing job I mentioned that someone dictated into the computer? It had me close to tearing my hair out. (Bald patches in a woman my age are very unbecoming. Thank goodness for cold weather and stocking caps.)

Why was this book so hard to edit? Total lack of punctuation. No periods to indicate the stop of a sentence, no commas to indicate phrasing. Do you know how **hard** it is to figure out what someone is trying to say, without punctuation to indicate phrasing and where thoughts end?

I spent hours trying to find the train of thought, where one sentence ended and another started. After I inserted punctuation, then I fixed grammar and spelling. I couldn't tell if the words/spelling were right until I knew what the author was trying to say. It was exhausting. All because the author didn't use punctuation -- a simple period -- or capitalize the start of each new sentence.

- ✓ *Do Yourself A Favor*: If you didn't master the basics of writing in elementary school, do it **now**. Learn punctuation. Learn capitalization. Learn sentence structure. Learn spelling. These are the mechanics. Another way of looking at it: your weapons in the battlefield of publishing.

How do you do that?

Read.
Read.
Read.
Read. (get the picture?)

Read lots of books, big books, bestsellers, classics. **Pay attention** to how authors put sentences together. **Pay attention** to how punctuation is used. Learn grammar through *example*.

Writing is war, and with e-publishing and self-publishing exploding, there are a whole lot more soldiers and armies in the battle, competing for readers. You want to go out there with the most effective weapons possible -- not a bunch of spitballs.

Do Yourself a Favor: Tips and Quips on the Writing Life

SOMETHING TO SAY -- BUT *SHOULD* YOU?

You believe you have something to say. It's burning in your gut. Your mind races with images and words. Your heart pounds with righteous indignation or the glee of some mind-blowing discovery. Or a piece of advice you're sure will change the world. Or a story you just know everyone will enjoy. It is imperative, a matter of life-and-death, for you to communicate that teaching or revelation or story, because time is of the essence. (Kind of like that scene from **Hitchhiker's Guide to the Galaxy**. A young woman had the solution to all the strife on Earth, but before she could tell someone, Earth got blown up for an inter-galactic bypass.)

In my editing work, I've come across lots of books *trying* to say something their authors believe must be communicated to the world. It matters greatly to them -- but does that automatically mean it *will* matter to anyone beyond them or their small circle of friends and co-workers?

Just because it's the most important thing in the world to you, does that mean everyone else in the world will -- or must -- feel the same way?

In too many books I've edited, the author starts out saying essentially, "I've learned valuable lessons in my lifetime, and I'm passing them on to you. I'm going to teach you how to avoid my mistakes." Then the author proceeds to go through his life story in excruciating detail of every mistake she made, every wrong other people inflicted on him. Nine (maybe nine-and-a-half) times out of ten, the author neglects to tell **how** she solved her problems. Nowhere does he say, "Here's where I went wrong. These are the warning signs. This is what you need to do differently." Or stop doing.

This may just be my opinion, but blaming other people and wallowing in your misery might not be a good plan. It might make you feel good, might bring closure to your life pain, but how exactly is that helping <u>other</u> people? If you want to teach people something, focus on solutions and lessons to share. The positive part of the story. Don't keep your revelations locked inside your head, and expect people to figure it out by watching you stumble for 200 pages.

Sorry, but there are more than enough books full of misery with no solutions. The world doesn't need more people pointing out what's wrong with the government or the economy or your neighbor's back yard or the church down the street -- with no suggestions for **how to fix** those problems. Were you as disgusted as I was, during a past presidential election, when one candidate said, essentially, "My opponent's plan won't work. My plan will fix this country within a few years of my being elected," and yet he **refused** to give even a hint of what his plan was? Reporters and other candidates asked the big selfish jerk point-blank what his plan was, and he refused to tell! What good does that do anyone?

You believe you have something to say, but if all you're doing is wallowing without offering any concrete lessons, any solid advice to your readers, it's better to just keep silent.

What's the difference between a wise man who keeps his mouth shut, and a fool who keeps his mouth shut? **Nobody knows!**

Do Yourself a Favor: Tips and Quips on the Writing Life

WHOSE RULES? MASTER THE RULES BEFORE YOU BREAK THEM

For a while, I had a "co-worker" who was driving me nuts -- or at least, driving me to empty my chocolate stash.

"Co-worker" is in quotes because while we did work for the same publishing company, we had never met, and I didn't even know his/her name. When I received books to edit, her assessment of the book came with it, with recommendations for the level of editing and what needed fixing.

Grrrrrrr! I just wanted to reach through the assessment and throttle her sometimes. She insisted on rules that honestly made no sense.

"Paragraphs should **always** be between 7 and 10 lines. No more. No less."

"**Never** start a sentence with a conjunction -- rewrite all sentences that start with 'and' and 'but' so they read properly."

"Non-fiction books should **never** have more than five exclamation marks. Any more than that and they will lose their impact."

Seriously? Only five exclamation marks among 85,000 words? Just how do you decide what sentences are such a high priority that they deserve those rare punctuation marks? Who decided that punctuation needs to be rationed so severely?

Granted, too many exclamation marks do lose their effectiveness. Recently I edited a book where I swear the author used an exclamation mark every other sentence. Bleah!

She made more statements in a similar vein, which never seemed to make any sense when I actually read the book and caught the rhythm and flavor and **style** of the author's voice. See, that's the thing -- those "corrections" she demanded would change the author's voice. And I just think that's wrong. (See? I started a sentence with a conjunction, and I solemnly swear no lightning bolt came down from the sky and hit my fingers on the keyboard.)

I had a publisher who applied *business rules* of writing to *fiction*, and that just didn't work. She insisted ellipses were "illegal" and took them out of dialog where "..." indicated someone was trailing off and hadn't finished the sentence/thought. ("I don't know," she said, "what if ..." turned into. "I don't know," she said, "what if." Huh???) It made no sense -- but she insisted ellipses were illegal. Yeah, in the business world, but not in fiction dialog!

Paragraphs need to be as long -- or as short -- as necessary to suit the rhythm, the feel, the voice of the piece. Paragraphs need to be long enough to complete their purpose. Such as creating a word picture, setting a scene, maybe even slowing down the pace of the story at that point and generating an emotion.

Some paragraphs are only one sentence long -- they are short to put emphasis on a statement.

Some paragraphs fill up the whole page, maybe two pages, until they convey the image the writer wants to create or the information the author needs to convey, or slows down the pace. Don't break a thought apart into multiple pieces just because you've reached the maximum number of sentences some self-appointed arbiter of "rightness" has declared.

Granted, when you're in school and your teacher gives you guidelines, you **follow** them. When you're writing for a publisher, you follow their guidelines. When my publisher does not want sentences to start with "and" or "but," I comply. Yet when I'm writing for my own purposes and for other publishers, I don't have to follow that publisher's rules.

Cue: evil laughter. Now that I'm a publisher, I can establish my own rules, and if I say that starting a sentence with "and" or "but" is legal, then nobody can argue with me. If I say that you can have one-sentence paragraphs or forty-sentence paragraphs, nobody can tell me I'm wrong. *Mwah hah hah!*

Sentences start with conjunctions to put **emphasis** on something. Or to continue a thought. (See what I did there?) And even to establish a rhythm. Like poetry, but without the forced rhyme and meter.

Starting the writing journey, you need to learn the rules *until you figure out how words work together*, what function they perform in the sentence, and how to modify them -- just like when you set out across country, you refer to a map or use a GPS so you reach your destination. **But**, once you learn how to make the words work together, then you can break those rules to make your point, just like you can discard the maps once you are familiar with the route and surrounding countryside. When you learn the terrain, then you can go exploring.

In the case of writing, that means following a new discovery you made about your characters, or go off on a tangent. Having a planned route and destination for the story, knowing where you need to end up, gives you the freedom to wander, as long as you're still heading in the right direction.

Or in the case of construction on the highway (you wrote yourself into a hole or some brainstorm hit, such as killing off a main character) that forces you to take detours, you can adjust your route. You might end up with a more entertaining story by doing the crazy things that hit you like a bolt out of the blue, and require big changes. (What do you do if you decide to kill off the character who's supposed to be the villain -- or the hero? If you know where the story needs to end up, you can build a new road, find an off-ramp or on-ramp, and get back on track.)

As I've said before (warned you there'd be repetition!): You have to learn the rules and prove you have mastered them before you can break them. How do I know? Some of the biggest-selling authors break the rules all the time, but they keep selling. (Yeah, well, when **you** sell as well as they do, then you can write your own way.) Figure skaters have compulsive routines -- specific sequences of moves they must perform in competition, no argument allowed. Then they have routines where they can make up the sequence. If they do what they want and ignore the requirements, what they created might be pretty, but they still get scored low and even penalized. They must do the required routines to prove they know what they are doing. After that, they can go on to be creative and have fun. If you want to be a professional skater, good enough to compete (See the metaphor? Good enough to sell.), you need to know how to skate, what works and what doesn't and what will get you a broken leg, before you can start making up fancy moves and tricks. Make sense?

Same with writing. Prove you know what you're doing, and then people will trust you to try tricks that nobody else is using.

Michelle L. Levigne

PLOTTERS VS. PANTSERS

Ah, yes, the great debate -- should you plot or should you write by the seat-of-your-pants? Both sides of the debate can get rather rabid, even nasty, advocating for what they believe is the right (and only) way to write that novel.

You know what? It's **their** right way, and just because it's the way your favorite writer writes doesn't necessarily mean it has to be **your** right way.

Plotters: Planning out the sequence of events, the scenes, who is in each scene, what elements of the plot are introduced, complicated, resolved, advanced, whatever. Sometimes even how many pages or even words will be in the chapter or scene. Some people are so detailed, by the time they finish their outline, the book is mostly written. Some people have twenty-page, even thirty-page outlines for their books. Sitting down to write that book without knowing what's going to happen, to whom, and exactly on what page gives them hives. And the inverse is true -- those people give **me** hives.

Pantsers: The seat-of-the-pants writers. The ones who start out with just an idea, an image in their heads, or a question they want to explore. They might start with one character or an intriguing scene, and take it from there. (Tolkein started the whole Lord of the Rings and Hobbit phenomenon with a line that just came to him about a hole in the ground and a Hobbit who lived there. He had no idea what a Hobbit was when he started writing, but finding out revolutionized the fantasy genre. IMHO.) Such authors are only a few pages ahead of the readers in knowing whatever is going on in the book. They couldn't write by an outline -- they couldn't *write* an outline -- to save their lives. They'd rather chew glass than use an outline.

Okay, if those methods, and the different variations and extremes work for you, then **go for it**!

If neither sounds like what you want to do, and you have different ideas of how to organize your book -- or not organize it -- before you write it, then do that. **This is your baby**. Nobody has the right to tell you your baby is ugly ... **to a point**. There are some rules you need to follow, some forms you have to adhere to. It's an ugly truth, but must be faced if you're going to succeed as an author, because you have to be honest with yourself before anyone else: if a publisher doesn't want a book that looks like a baby with two sets of arms but no legs, and a head that looks forward and a second head that looks backwards, that's the publisher's choice. (Can we say Dr. Frankenstein? Or maybe Franken-Fido? *The Goodies*, anyone?) The crazy thing might just work! However, it's going to take a lot of work and a lot of risk and effort to find the publisher who shares your vision and *does* want to take a risk on Frankenstein Jr.'s creation. I'm just warning you.

- ✓ *Do Yourself A Favor:* see the other chapters on following the rules, deciding what rules to follow and what rules to chuck to the side of the road, and learning the what and why and how of those rules before you surgically remove them from your creation.

Me ... I'm a *plontser*. I'm in the middle. I know where I want the journey of my story to go and where I want it to end. I have some general ideas of the important turning points, the highs and lows, the complications in my book, but very little beyond that. *Sometimes.* Sometimes, if I'm writing in an established universe, I have a lot of details, a lot of background, and I have to write within the lines because I referred to these events or that character's life in a previous book. <u>Consistency is vital for survival.</u> Don't start a story with a blue-eyed hero, who somehow ends up with brown eyes, or three eyes, by the final page. (I edited a story once where a chase scene started with the hero in a beat-up blue pickup truck, but by the time he cornered the villain in an alley, his pickup truck had morphed into a black SUV. Unless you're writing urban fantasy with magical shapeshifting spells hitting at random intervals, that sort of thing won't work. Trust me on this!)

Sometimes, though, I start off with an outline of less than a page, with very vague details. Maybe I don't even know the villain's name, or the name of the town/planet where the story takes place -- but I learn those things as I go along, like a movie playing inside my head -- and I get a 400-page book after starting out with a one-page outline. I give myself the freedom to go off on tangents, to follow rabbit trails, to explore -- and to rewrite that outline if it stifles me. I definitely have to change that outline if my characters, who are becoming more three-dimensional as I get deeper into the story, suddenly dig their heels in and say, "Nuh uh, ain't goin' there -- I wanna do *this*, not what you have planned for me."

Yes, that happens sometimes. Not as often as I'd like! And when it does, that is the most fun! It's like the story is *writing itself.* Sometimes I get stories like that, where everything that happens just makes sense, and I always know at least four scenes ahead of time what's going to happen, what needs to happen, and that helps me write the scenes leading up to that moment, which makes for a lot less rewriting later. Always a good thing to avoid.

Don't argue with your characters. Change your characters, rewrite your characters, do brain surgery and plastic surgery if necessary, but don't waste your time and energy arguing with them and then making them do something that is *totally wrong for the character <u>as he or she is written now</u>. If you make your characters do and say things that aren't "right" for them without changing their programming and backgrounds and secret pains and dreams, your readers will know and they won't be happy. Characters who are untrue to themselves are TSTL, in writer's shorthand:* **Too Stupid To Live.**

The point of all this (this repetition is for your own good!) is that you have to **write by the method that works** for **you**, not what other people in your writing group, your critique group, your creative writing class advocate. Do what works for you.

The mechanics are set, non-negotiable rules. (Of course, that doesn't mean you follow the rules when you're writing dialog if you need to illustrate the type of person your character is. Make sense? Bad grammar is a way of showing rather than telling.) The standards and guidelines established by the publisher you write for are also non-negotiable. Everything else? That's up to you. The story is an exploration of *your* private world, so that means the equipment you take with you, the path you follow through that world, is entirely up to you. After all, just because your favorite trail guide specializes in desert treks doesn't mean you have to use desert-compatible equipment when you're going through the rainforest. The same applies with writing. Adapt to suit the story. Adapt to suit **your** soul. Be a plotter, a pantser, or a plontser, to whatever degree necessary. And don't let anybody tell you you're wrong.

DECISIONS BEFORE YOU GET STARTED

I don't care how much of a pantser you are, there are some decisions you must make before you start writing. Even if it's just a few minutes before you open up a new document in the computer or open up a notebook to start scribbling.

POV: what point of view are you going to use?

First person -- I, me

Second person -- you

Third person -- he, him, her, she, they

Yes, you can have several points of view within the book, just make sure that it is **clear** to readers when you shift from Frank's POV to Helen's. Be kind to your readers and do it at scene changes, or at the start of a new chapter. Make it clear in the first sentence, whenever possible, that the POV has indeed changed.

- ✓ *Do Yourself a Favor*: avoid everything and anything that will confuse your readers or irritate them, and give them an excuse to put the book down and never pick it up again. Or worse, throw it against the wall, out the window, or in the toilet. And then get online and rant about what a stupid book it was and what a bad writer you are.

Would they really do that to you? People nowadays are willing to stab someone because their fast-food order was wrong. You tell me.

I don't know how many books I've edited, where a scene starts and people are talking, and not only is there no indication of **who these people are**, no dialog tags, no indication of where the scene takes place or the time of day, or how soon after the last scene it starts, but no indication of whose eyes are being used as the camera to record the scene. That's POV -- the camera recording the scene.

Example:

"Hi."

"Oh, hi. What's up?"

"Oh, you know. The usual. Did you hear if Fred's coming over?"

"No. Why would we expect him?"

"Oh, you know Fred, he thinks he has to be involved in everything."

"Even worse than him is Curtis. At least his feelings get hurt enough when he's not automatically included, he sits at home and sulks, and won't come around until you apologize."

"How can we apologize when he doesn't tell us that we did anything wrong?"

"Exactly. If we're lucky, he stays away forever."

Okay, how many people are in the conversation?
Where does it take place?
What time of day?
Through whose eyes do we see this?
We don't know because the author didn't bother telling us!

Try this again, with dialog tags and some set dressing:
Marvin muffled a sigh into a silent grumble as Jake sauntered into the back room. Until that moment, he had been happily working on tallying their gate receipts for the night.

What did this bozo want now? Was he going to pretend he had second thoughts and wanted to be part of the Concert Garden, now that opening night was a big success? Marvin bent his head over his work and hoped Jake would think he didn't see him.

"Hi." Gretchen's voice startled him. He looked toward the door, and grinned to see Jake jump, startled at her entrance. Just how long was he planning on standing there until he was noticed?

"Oh, hi. What's up?" Marvin tucked the handful of twenties into the cash box, then moved it off the chair, a silent invitation to her.

"Oh, you know. The usual. Did you hear if Fred's coming over?"

"No. Why would we expect him?" Jake said with a sneer.

"Oh, you know Fred, he thinks he has to be involved in everything." Gretchen turned her head enough that Jake couldn't see her expression as she rolled her eyes.

"Even worse than him is Curtis. At least his feelings get hurt enough when he's not automatically included, he sits at home and sulks, and won't come around until you apologize."

"How can we apologize when he doesn't tell us that we did anything wrong?"

"Exactly. If we're lucky, he stays away forever." Marvin glared at Jake, and wished he would take the hint.

Do you have an idea now of where this is taking place, and when, and whose eyes are recording this scene? Maybe even some hints of relationships and feelings toward different characters? (Without an info-dump, I might add.)

Choose your POV character. Stick with him or her. And for the sake of your readers, don't head-hop. (That's discussed elsewhere.)

Genre:
Know what kind of book you're writing. Do some research into the

expectations and descriptions of the various standard genres. Yes, you can mix a few genres, but not to excess, and not to the point of ridiculous.

For instance: Heavy-metal Western set during the Stone Age.

Nuh uh. Not going to work -- unless it's maybe a comedy with an overall cover of science fiction, say a malfunctioning time machine, in which a heavy metal band gets yanked through time, mostly in a Western setting, with short visits to the Stone Age.

Just saying.

- ✓ *Do Yourself A Favor*: learn the accepted parameters of the genres out there. For your early books, stay within those parameters. When you've built up a reputation, when readers trust you, then you can start stretching the envelope. Slowly. Don't burst the envelope -- unless you're that kind of wacky genius talent that can completely shatter the envelope, mix it with a few other envelopes, and come up with a totally new genre that it will take several generations before someone comes up with an appropriate name for it. Granted, you think you're that kind of talent now, but do you really want to take the chance and make yourself such a humongous laughingstock that no one will ever read you again?

This goes back to what I've said multiple times here: learn the rules, learn why they are there, learn how they work, before you violate them.

Note: when someone asks you what you write, don't say, "I'm working on a fictional novel."

Besides being redundant (it's understood that a novel IS fiction) you'll mark yourself as an amateur who knows pretty close to nothing about the lingo of writing, and you probably flunked a few English classes in there somewhere.

Genres (a short, sampling list, certainly not all-inclusive):
Romance (and all the sub-genres)
Fantasy
Science Fiction
Historical
Suspense
True Crime
Mystery
Comedy
Drama
Erotica
Western
Fictionalized History/Alternate History

Biblical
Inspirational
Spiritual Warfare
Magical Realism
General Fiction (what the elitists would prefer to call "literature" -- which for me just means it's about stuff going on in the present, maybe some crises of an emotional nature, and you can't really slap a label on it. If you could slap a label on it, it would be under one of the other divisions.)

Then there are the subdivisions among all those genres, depending on the age level of the audiences:
Juvenile or Children's
Middle-Grade
Young Adult
New Adult
Adult

Someone once asked what the difference was between "genre" fiction and "literary" fiction.
I loved the answer:
*In genre fiction, something **happens**. People change. Challenges arise. Problems are dealt with. Society changes. People fight for something and either win or lose. There's failure or success, sometimes both.*
In literary fiction ... people think a lot and feel a lot, but there's no growth, no learning. At the end, after a lot of angst and thinking and debating ... nothing much has changed, if anything has changed at all.
'Nuff said?

Research:
Please, please, please do your research if you're writing about anything set in the past, in a place where you don't live (or haven't lived in a long time), a place you've never visited, or dealing with technology or a culture that is not your own.
I know research can be boring. But consider this: If it bores you to look up information about the place where you're setting your story, or the technology that's vital to the action, or the culture that your hero comes from ... *maybe you shouldn't be writing about them in the first place?* If it bores you, readers are going to pick up on that, and be bored, too. Or they might interpret your boredom as arrogance, and decide you have an attitude problem, and stop reading.

✓ *Do Yourself A Favor*: Never hack off readers. Never give them an excuse to close the book. They might not pick it up again. Irritate them enough, they'll tell other people not to waste their time and money. You don't want that!

I edited a book once that took place on a Polynesian island in the late 1800s. The author, looking through the heroine's eyes (an uneducated island girl), described a box as being about the size of a Kleenex box. I checked for the dates and Kleenex wasn't making boxed tissues during the time of the story. In another place, the author talked about bodies of plague victims being wrapped in black plastic bags before burial. Umm, nope, they didn't have black plastic bags back then. Five minutes searching "tissue boxes" or "Kleenex" or "plastic bags" on the Internet could have avoided those very obvious anachronisms.

Other people have talked about the disconnect they get, the mental "clank" that occurs when they were reading an otherwise wonderfully written book, and they come across a detail that they know, because they live in the area, could not be there. A bird in the wrong part of the country. A flower blooming in the wild either too late or too early in the season, or not belonging in that part of the country at all. A car chase that specifically mentions two-way traffic on a one-way street, and to make matters worse, crossing several streets that do not intersect with that street in real life.

Okay, you can get away with some of these anomalies if you're writing fantasy or alternate history, and you state that the plant life and animal life and migratory habits and the layout of city streets are different in the world you've created ... but do you want to have to rely on that excuse all the time?

Do the research. Don't be lazy.

Before I close this rant, I must mention a corollary to the research accuracy problem:

Self-appointed experts who did no research, and yet insist, loudly, that what happened in your story could not have happened, or did not happen. Don't get into arguments with them if you can at all avoid it, because they will insist that you are wrong *even when you show them your research*. Why? Because it conflicts with *their* idea of reality, or what they choose to believe is scientific fact. Remember the old phrase: *Fact is stranger than fiction*? Well, friends of mine have run into enough conflicts with self-appointed know-it-alls, to know the truth of this. One was told that a Civil War post-battle scene could not possibly have happened. Yet when she shared the scans she had made from a genuine Civil War diary, relating the exact same event in her story, the self-appointed expert insisted my friend should still cut it from the book, because nobody would believe it.

So that's something to consider when you do your research. Be ready to stick to your guns, when people argue with your historically accurate scenes and details. Be ready to defend yourself. At the same time, pick your battles carefully. Don't we have enough experience with politics nowadays to know that what people *want* to believe is always stronger than actual facts and the truth? Be ready to have an alternate scene that accomplishes the same purpose, if someone with some authority and influence tells you it's best to cut that scene or detail, because nobody will believe it.

That's a fact that's regrettably stranger than fiction.

Do Yourself a Favor: Tips and Quips on the Writing Life

HUMILIATING CONFESSION TIME

Or

ORGANIZATION, PREPARATION, and MULTITASKING -- THE LIFE YOU SAVE COULD BE YOUR OWN

Also known as: Learn from My Mistakes (and if I catch anyone snickering, you'll end up in my next book, and you won't enjoy it!)

Disaster. Tragedy. Frustration. Messed up organization -- or an unreasonable facsimile.

I had a book due March 1. I *thought* I was way ahead of schedule. I turned in the manuscript at the start of February, giving me the rest of the month to devote to pulling another book out of storage to revise and turn in to another publisher. Again, ahead of schedule. (Not so fast with the celebration and patting myself on the back...)

Part of the responsibility of authors at my former publisher was to format: insert the cover page and copyright information and about-the-author info before we turned in the book. I copied and pasted all that information from the previous book in the series, and as I glanced through the list of titles, I caught a big mistake.

The book due March 1 was *another* title altogether in the series.

I had reversed the sequence of titles.

Not a good scenario, with less than three weeks left to turn in the right book.

Fortunately, the book that was due was one I had had in my files for years, revised and polished multiple times. It didn't need much work at all to make it ready to turn in.

Whew!

The up side to this disaster was that I had both contracted books done for the year. I could concentrate on other books and get ahead (hah!) on my due dates.

But I wouldn't have had a "rescue" in this disaster if I hadn't done gobs of planning and working ahead, which is what many writers advocate: Write the book, put it aside, work on something else, come back to it and revise, put it aside, work on something else, come back to it, etc.

- ✓ *Do Yourself a Favor*: (granted, something that is really only applicable several years into your writing career) Always have several projects in various stages of roughing, revising, and polishing. If you can manage it, avoid focusing solely on one project from start to finish. You might turn around one day and realize that you thought you were on schedule for one deadline, but another book was actually due.

When I have a series planned, I take time to rough draft the whole series. If I can. When I got my contract for that particular series of books, I made sure I had time and then rough drafted all eight books. (I was already ahead of the game because two of the eight had been written, as stand-alones, and revised at least two times.) This let me know what was going to happen, so I could make reference to what else was going on in the town where the books were set, when events overlapped from one book to another. This also let me foreshadow what would happen from one book to the next, when I went back and started making revisions. This is a very helpful thing -- it avoids the tragedy of writing yourself into a corner and contradicting yourself because you said one thing in Book 1, but by the time you got to Book 4, the event or the people involved or the props weren't there anymore!

Always look ahead. Always plan ahead. Take projects in small bites. Work ahead. Never fall for the line that, "Deadline pressure makes me *soooooooo* creative and productive!" Nuh uh. The only thing deadline pressure guarantees is gray hair, stress-related trouble, nervous eating disorders, and no rescue in sight when you mess up. Plan ahead. The writing life you save will be your own.

Yes, this seems contradictory, coming from someone who leans more toward the pantser side of the plontser hybrid style of writing. Like I've said before and will say many times again: *do and use and apply what works*. Don't let rules paralyze or hobble or smother you. Just because plotting and writing outlines gives you hives doesn't mean you can't plan ahead. Just do it your way.

THAT IDEA STORE

Anyone who proclaims themselves to be writers, whether they actually write or not, always get hit with this question: **Where Do You Get Your Ideas?**

For a little while, I had a smart-alec answer: There's this little shop in the French Quarter in New Orleans...

But no, you really can't buy ideas.

You have to harvest them.

Scavenge them.

Make yourself open to being "attacked" by them.

Even "steal" or "borrow" them from other writers and then perform plastic surgery until they become identifiably yours.

That means you often toss away everything from the original idea, sculpting and cutting and grafting in (yes, I'm mixing my metaphors) until it becomes a new creature. If you do your work right, it won't rebel and turn on you like Frankenstein's monster. Then again, sometimes the most fun I've had while writing has been when my characters became so real that they did what they darn well wanted to, and not what was on the road map of my sketchy plot. (Which is why my plots and synopses and whatever are sometimes very, very sketchy at the beginning -- to give lots of wiggle room and opportunity to go off on tangents.) Setting up your characters and situations and sitting back and watching them perform is the best fun!

Ideas are -- after all this time, I am thoroughly convinced -- living things. They latch onto you and nag you and invade your dreams and like spoiled children, pull you away from your current work-in-progress to listen to them **now**!

You have to tame them. That means letting them nag and interrupt your sleep and your social time, but only enough to write down what they're saying. Do not let your ideas drag you over to the computer or notepad or whatever you use for your first draft to sit down **now** and start writing their story. Because here's the secret: The ideas aren't sure what their story is, either. Not when they're first born. They need to grow up and figure out what they are supposed to do in your head. You have to let them keep talking, keep nagging, keep playing in the back of your mind. Let them bring friends along -- in fact, you should wait and even pretend to ignore them, until they bring friends to make more noise and really catch hold of your attention. That's when the story starts taking on multiple layers, adds complications, goes from black-and-white to color, and gets a soundtrack. So to speak. If you start telling your idea's story too soon, you'll stall out, and your idea might even abandon you just after the big explosive, "Hey, look at me!" start. Why? Because you gave the idea what it wanted -- your attention -- too soon in the process. You have to make it wait and grow and learn what most of the story is before you start writing. (No, you don't have to have the whole thing clear in your head, just enough to know what some of the barriers and complications and supporting actors are.) Make the idea fight for your time and attention, and it won't abandon you. It's worked too darn hard to have a hissy at you and walk away now!

Do Yourself a Favor: Tips and Quips on the Writing Life

THE PERILS AND PITFALLS AND PLUSSES OF WRITING -- OR THINKING OF WRITING -- A SERIES

Yes, almost all of my books belong in one series or another. It's kind of a disease, or maybe a manifestation of OCD. I can't help it. When I create a situation, a town, a star-spanning civilization, a cast of characters, give them history, and create a sense of continuing with their lives after the final page ... more story ideas just come.

Or in the case of the Tabor Heights and Commonwealth Universe books, I wrote a bunch of individual books, and after a certain point in the revision process, I made connections. If I change the family name of this character, or tweak some historical events in the lives of these characters, or this planet, and I connect them at these different points in the history of the town, or the storyline, change the name of the lawyer in this book to the name of the lawyer in another book, and make this guy a cousin of this girl and ...

See what I mean?

Suddenly, all these connections came together, and I had a 1000-year span of history in a SF universe, and a series of interconnected and overlapping stories about the congregation of one church in a small Northeast Ohio town. It came together kind of organically, I guess you could say.

But it all goes back to not just planning, but being familiar enough with your stories and your characters, their geography, their histories, their relationships, that you can tweak and reconnect, change names, reorganize timelines, and tie them all together.

These stories series just kind of grew together. Along the way, I was able to bring in other stories that I only had notes for, thumbnail sketches of the events to take place or the quest to complete. With the solid foundation of the already-existing stories, and the timeline and history and cast of characters established, it helped me figure out where the new stories and characters fit into the series. Even more important, I knew what *had to* happen in the story, so it fit with what went before and after it, or what could not happen, because someone else made that discovery or defeated that enemy, or the enemy had to grow more powerful for a few more books or ... see what I mean? The more solid the overall tapestry of the story universe, the more certain I became about what had to happen, and how, and to whom.

Planning, but not exactly the kind of detail-oriented, nitpicky, anal-retentive planning that gives pantsers hives. This is more along the lines of familiarity with a landscape, with a map, with the boundaries -- and then giving yourself the freedom to run around within those boundaries. You can still have fun. Just like setting up a fence and putting up playground equipment and mulch or other protective ground cover may restrict the children at recess in some ways, but at the same time sets them free to run around and have fun and even take silly risks. Yeah, a slide only three feet off the ground may be wimpy, but a kid is then free to run up the slide and stand at the top without fear of breaking his neck. A little girl can pump with all her might on the swings, because she knows if she loses her grip at the top of the arch and slides off, she'll land on padding and only have a few bruises at worst.

At some point, you're going to need to create a map or a timeline or cast of characters, with an accompanying chart or list of descriptions and relationships, so things you say in chapter four don't contradict what you told readers in chapter one. Recently I edited a book where the author stated some of the heroes of his book were Vietnam veterans, and the story took place in the present. Problem: the nephew of one of the heroes was born just after he came back from Vietnam, he was considered a "boy," and the uncle worried about losing custody of him. If the author had set up a timeline to keep track of people's ages and when certain events happened, he would have realized that the "boy" had to be at least forty-three years old!

- ✓ *Do Yourself A Favor*: Take notes as you write the book, if you're a pantser. Take notes as you write even if you're a plotter, because you might just decide what you've created as you're writing makes more sense than the details you plotted out ahead of time. Take notes and make sure they're handy to refer to, so you don't contradict yourself.

I once read a fan fiction story where Remington Steele was involved in a car chase, and in the space of maybe three pages, the makes and colors of both cars changed multiple times. Sometimes Steele was doing the chasing, and sometimes he was being chased. Don't do that to your readers!

Even pantsers have to do *some* planning, even if it's just after the fact, to coordinate everything. So what does this have to do with writing a series?

You need those notes to keep track of what happened in the previous book when you write a sequel. Or a third book. Or a fourth book. Or just plan them, to send a proposal to your editor or agent.

- ✓ *Do Yourself A Favor*: take DETAILED notes.

Do Yourself a Favor: Tips and Quips on the Writing Life

Confession time: In my Commonwealth Universe SF series, I'm filling in all the holes created when I just wrote the first dozen or so stories all over the place along the 1,000-year history. Some of that was caused by originally writing these books as stand-alones. For instance, I roughed what eventually became the middle book of the Chorillan Cycle, and then I wrote some of the Sunsinger books, and during the tweaking and connecting process, "discovered" that the hero of the Sunsinger books was the multi-great-grandfather of the heroine of the Chorillan books.

Anyway ... I'm filling in the holes in the Commonwealth books, and made the mistake of sending a list of titles and thumbnail sketches of the books to my publisher. She insists I'll have more sales if readers can read straight through the series from the beginning, and with no holes. (Booooooooring!) Yeah, well, she's the publisher, and I have to trust her, so I confessed to all the notes and tentative plans sitting in my computer. Now I'm committed (and sometimes I think I should have been committed years ago!) to writing those stories. And guess what happened? I *didn't* take detailed notes when I was writing about Leapers and mentioned the history of their ancestors, the Khybor race. (Leapers are female pilots who mentally link with their ships. They jump between dimensions to travel vast distances quickly without stealing or borrowing from the proprietary technology/terminology of other copyrighted and trademarked SF universes.) While writing the first draft of this book, I was also in the process of reading the previous six or seven books in the Commonwealth Universe and taking notes. This will help me rewrite the bad, contradictory rough draft of **First Law**. The Khybors basically thumb their noses at the Central Allied Worlds (a disintegrating galactic government, from the ashes of which the Commonwealth will rise) and take off for other universes to escape a lot of genetic cleansing and genocide and racial prejudice. When I sat down to do a second draft of **First Law**, I realized that I had contradicted some bits of technological and sociological history I had established in the first few books. Because, confession time again, it has been a year or two since I wrote anything in the Commonwealth.

How pitiful is that? The creator can't remember the names or ages or hobbies or favorite colors of her babies.

So take notes and make plans and keep things straight! Create a guidebook if you have to. Don't end up wasting a lot of time and having to reinvent the wheel multiple times, and irritate your longsuffering publisher with excuse after excuse after excuse. It's not good business, for one thing.

Books that can stand on their own are, in my opinion at least, a smart choice for new writers, or at least people still struggling to make that first big sale. The tide of opinion and taste keeps changing, up and down, on whether people want two-book, three-book, or even ten-book series. Be ready to hand that kind and generous editor who's willing to give you a chance a book that stands on its own. AND YET, leave the door open for more books that follow up on the main character, or the friends of the main character, or even just set in the same town or society or culture or galactic civilization.

When you finally "make it," chances are good someone in power at the publishing company will say, "So what else have you got?" Of course, that powerful person might ask that question even if they don't want to buy the book you're offering -- which means you've impressed them enough they're willing to give you another chance. Good for you!

Believe me, you want to be able to say, "Oh, I have another book rough drafted/finished/in the planning stages." Of course, then you need to be ready to at least give them an elevator pitch, summing up the general idea of the story in a few sentences.

So plan ahead. Be ready to pitch a book that will stand all on its lonesome, but have options for more stories. Never be a one-hit wonder. Even Margaret Mitchell had another project in the works.

Do Yourself a Favor: Tips and Quips on the Writing Life

ARE YOU READY?

✓ *Do Yourself A Favor*: ALWAYS be ready when inspiration strikes.

Problem: it strikes when you are <u>least</u> able to drop everything and take notes.

Big bad confession time: I get most of my great ideas ... in ***church***! Yeah, I sit there in the ten minutes before the service starts, or in my Sunday morning class, industriously taking notes, but not on my teacher's lesson. (Sorry, George!)

I don't know why it happens, but it just does. If I could figure out how to turn on the spigot, and control it, I would be in great shape.

So, you need to be ready to write down those ideas *when* they strike. I keep a notebook in my purse. I have a notepad sitting on my desk. My iPad sits on the table next to my bed -- very convenient for ideas that strike in the middle of the night, because I don't have to turn a light on, and it's a whole heck of a lot more legible than the notes I used to try to write in the dark. I have a small notebook I stick in the cup holder of the treadmill at the gym. When I'm out taking my morning walk, I use my iPhone to listen to Podcasts. (Podcasts about writing, first thing in the morning, are a great way to get the creative pump primed.) When I get an idea, often from whatever I'm listening to, my iPhone allows me to either tap notes into the Notes app, or I can dictate something in the voice recorder.

Use what works best for you. Notepad, iPad, voice recorder, whatever.

Don't depend on yourself to remember when you finally get a chance to write it down or put it in the computer an hour later. Write it down immediately when you get that flash of inspiration from an overheard bit of conversation or an advertisement or a commercial or a great scene in the movie. Something that perfectly filled in that gap in the story you're working on. Or you see a picture that reminds you of a character, and you realize your heroine's cousin is just perfect to say that silly line that gets things moving. You know what I mean, that "Ah ha!" moment when you feel like you're "remembering" something, but you're really just filling in the blank spots.

Yeah, you get great ideas when you're driving somewhere, or doing the laundry or cleaning the bathroom or working out or changing the baby's diapers or cooking dinner, and you just can't drop everything to write down the idea. Well, **Drop It** as soon as you can. Don't tell yourself you'll remember an hour from now, or five hours from now. Because you get distracted and you forget, and all you're left with is the sense that you had a great idea.

Be Ready.
Don't leave anything to chance. When inspiration sneaks up on you and whispers in your ear or whacks you across the back of the head, be ready to snare it before it runs away!

TOOLS, EDUCATION, AND SUPPORT:

Do Yourself a Favor: Tips and Quips on the Writing Life

WHO ARE YOU TALKING TO?

Eventually on the road to publication, every author gets hit with this question, in different forms:

WHO is your audience?

Big bad confession time: I usually hear crickets when someone asks me that question while I'm actually writing the story. I don't know the answer until after the book is polished and I'm trying to sell it. Maybe...

That's the problem with a lot of writers. We're just having too dang much fun writing the story, exploring our characters, creating them, making them real, winding them up and then throwing them into an obstacle course of story and villains and problems to solve. We don't think about who will enjoy reading the story when it's finished. Heck, we probably think somewhere along the line that *everybody* will like this book. We love it, right? Everybody will have fun with it.

Well, the sad, cold truth is that question MUST be answered. If you're lucky enough to have a publisher who will do some PR, the marketing department will want to know who the audience is. Most of the time, you are stuck doing your own marketing and publicity. Even more discouraging, if you're self-publishing and registering your ISBN numbers and filling out all those blank fields at the different online bookstores or aggregator sites, you'll get that question and others like it, too. Be ready to answer the questions.

Who is your audience?

Who will be most likely to read your book?

(Who will not enjoy this book? Knowing that might just be as important as knowing who will go bonkers over it and buy fifty copies to give their friends.)

What age group?

What demographic of income or education or culture will be most attracted to this book -- or offended by it?

You need to think of those things somewhere along the line of writing the book. Considering those questions could help you with revisions.

- ✓ *Do Yourself A Favor:* picture someone in your head who represents your optimal, most ideal audience and reader. Then, when you do revisions, consider if that scene will generate the desired effect in or get the desired response from your reader. Make him laugh? Make her cry? Make him fight not to barf? Make her cheer? Make her sigh? Make him squirm and look around and wonder if anyone knows what he's thinking? If you don't want those reactions, this is the time to make the changes in your story. You don't want to have to have an argument with an unhappy reader in a bookstore or on a public forum, trying to explain why the reader is *wrong* to have that particular reaction.

Just.
Don't.

(Hint: never tell readers they're wrong to react to your story the way they do. Your job is to ensure they react the way you want them to.)

I'm sure we've all heard some story of a writer who got into an argument with a disappointed reader, or someone who criticized what they wrote or said, or made fun of a cherished character or scene. The writer whose blog or a thread they started on a reader forum blew up overnight, with 5,000 hits in the space of a few days. Yeah, her name became a household word among readers of that genre, but was that the desired effect? Some household items are treasures, while others are downright disgusting. Work to be the former, not the latter. (And if you don't know what former and latter are … learn! That's part of your job description too, as a writer.)

So think about your audience now, while you're rough drafting or revising or polishing. Don't wait until the editor or the marketing department or the online form to upload your book asks that question. Focus on the people you want to reach and their desired reactions, while the book is still pliable and can be changed and refocused and reshaped.

Then guess what? No crickets when the time comes to answer that question.

Win-win all around. Your editor and marketing department will love you.

Do Yourself a Favor: Tips and Quips on the Writing Life
READ FOR YOUR CAREER

Besides learning the mechanics of grammar, spelling, punctuation, sentence structure and POV, the best advice I can give you is to **read** books about writing. And not just books about writing, but books written by people who have *proven* they know what they're doing.

Yeah, there are probably a lot of people out there who can offer you gobs of advice on how to write your book, how to come up with your ideas, how to plot, how to develop characters, how to determine POV, how to market, how to create tension ... but if they aren't *doing* it themselves, and proving they know what they're doing with actual sales ... if the only books they've written talk about *how to write* ... it's kind of like hiring someone who never put on sneakers to be your track coach, y'know? Can you really learn the techniques of painting, the instinctive knowledge that seeps into the blood, that's part muscle memory and part dreaming, from someone who never picked up a brush, but only *sells* the supplies at the local craft store?

I found and read and now recommend a book that should be a primer for those starting out, just to give them an idea of what is involved in the writing life -- discipline, differences in approach and attitude, differences in marketing, in creativity, in just the day-to-day drudgery.

Secrets Of Successful Writers: interviews with fifty published, selling authors, conducted and edited by Darrell Pitt.

"Fifty writers" means fifty different viewpoints and approaches to writing, marketing, craft, art, etc. Read and see how everybody handles their writing, and then use the advice that works for **you**. As I've said before, in different ways, and will say again before this rant is finished: *Never, never, ever let someone tell you the only way to be a writer is* **their** *way.* Listen to the pros, the ones who are in the trenches and selling and still struggling and learning. Think hard. Experiment. Then apply what works for you.

And let me repeat and re-emphasize -- READ.

Michelle L. Levigne

HOW TO LOSE WRITING CONTESTS

Warning: This is a rant. I regularly judge a short writing contest for a publisher. People have to prove they can write, write well, and they have something to say -- with the prize being a publishing contract.

Want to lose this contest?

1) **Ignore proper grammar, spelling, and punctuation.** Use no commas, forget the closing quote marks in dialog, put question marks and exclamation points *outside* the quotes in dialog. Or what's even better, put the question marks/exclamation points at the end of the sentence, when the dialog ended half a sentence ago. ("How can you say that to me" she wailed?)

2) **Don't re-read your entry before hitting the "send" button.** Don't take any time to look for missing words, or errors in spelling and punctuation and grammar. Don't make sure sentences are complete and you actually made your point before you ran out of words/space.
2a) **Expect the judge to read your mind** and judge you on what you meant to say, rather than what you actually said.

3) **PLEASE USE ALL CAPITALS.** Hurt the judge's eyes by writing in all capitals -- the equivalent of shouting.

4) **Promise the readers they're going to learn about something – and then don't deliver.** Give the piece a title that has nothing whatsoever to do with the contents of your essay. Start out with a maudlin story about some sad event in your life, and then in the final paragraph quote a Bible verse with nothing to indicate what the verse has to do with the story -- and expect the judge to know what you forgot to say. Or better yet, catch their interest with a cute story about a dog or someone's kid or your beloved grandmother, then at about the three-quarters mark, change the subject entirely, and go from memoir to diatribe on a topic totally unrelated to where you started. Yes, eventually the two totally different mental pathways will converge, but about 5,000 words beyond your word limit. Again, you are expecting the judge to read your mind and judge you on what wasn't included in the entry.

5) **Waste your word count talking about the book you want to get published, while avoiding proving you can write.** Talk about your life story (liberally sprinkled with bad grammar, spelling and punctuation) for

about three-quarters of your word limit. Then in the final paragraph tell the judge you have a novel you want to publish that has nothing to do with your life story. Talk about the ministry you want to have, that you can launch if you get a book published, while proving you have no communication skills whatsoever.

5a) At the very end of the entry, admit you haven't even written the story yet. Broadly hint that you expect the publishing package prize to include someone to write it for you.

5b) **Use emotional blackmail or bullying.** Claim God told you to enter the contest. Write a paragraph about winning the contest and how great it'll be for your ministry, without saying what the book is about or what your ministry is. Claim God dictated the book to you (umm, NO. My God uses proper grammar, spelling and punctuation -- and you didn't) and promised you would win because there are souls out there *only you* can save. (Not God -- you will save them.) Judges love it when you try to make God a bully so you can win. Wouldn't it save time and effort if God just sent the publisher to your front door with a contract and a ghost writer?

6) **Ignore the rules of the contest** -- word count, deadlines, submission format, etc. If the rules say entries must only be in English, then yes, please, submit your story in a foreign language. Chances are good the judges, who only speak English, will be intimidated and let you win, in fear that you will sue for discrimination. By all means, go over the word count limits. If the limit is 800, send 1,500 words, or even 3,000. Judges can't tell, just by looking at the submission screen, that you sent too much. If the rules say to either paste your entry into the submission screen, or attach a Word document to the email, then by all means, attach a PDF or even a desktop publishing file to the email, with the entire book included. If the rules specifically state text only, then yes, please, include illustrations. Or even a soundtrack/MP3 file! Or even better, tell the judges you have a great book about a dog/cat/missions trip/church scandal/divine retribution, and if they're interested in publishing it, they should write to you and you'll send the entire manuscript.

7) **Wait until the last minute.** If the contest has been going on for ten days, wait until the end of the tenth day to submit, so the judges are overwhelmed by a tsunami of entries. Better yet, wait until 11:45pm, when the contest site closes down at midnight.

7a) **Ignore the fact that the longer you wait, the more judges will compare your story** to what they read before. It doesn't matter that you have to be **better** than what they've already read, to get into the "worth a second read" file.

8) **Waste your word limit**. Spend the first 750 words of your contest entry talking about what a horrible life you led, how sinful you were, how people abused you. Then in words 751-780, relate how your neighbor/mother/grandmother/boss/probation officer nagged until you came to church. Then from words 781 to 850 (because your story is just so unique, the judges won't hold it against you if you go over the 800-word limit) declare that once you met Jesus, everything was magically changed and God gave you a ministry, so you need to win the contest to publish your book that hasn't even been written yet, so you can expand your ministry -- without stating what that ministry is.

Hint: The story you want to tell isn't about your awful, miserable life before you met Jesus. Your story is how your life changed once you surrendered to Jesus, the process and the struggle and everything you learned. That's the story you need to share. That's the story people want to hear. Don't cheat them by implying that everything gets fixed in one fell swoop the moment they say yes to Jesus. Because you know that isn't true. The end of the story is not getting saved -- that's just the beginning, the launching point of the real story.

- ✓ *Do Yourself A Favor*: Read the rules. Learn the rules. Follow the rules. Figure out what the real story is, the story you would want to hear if someone else was telling it. Then tell it!

Do Yourself a Favor: Tips and Quips on the Writing Life

PRACTICE WHAT YOU PREACH WHILE YOU'RE PREACHING

You know what really ticks me off?

Writing books, or articles on writing, where the authors make mistakes.

(Chances are good I made some stupid mistakes here in this book, and you caught them. I swear, I proofread, and my co-editor proofread, and I had a few people beta read, to tame down the snark factor and catch those stupid typos. Once long ago, I pulled out a story I had written years before, and read, "She sat on his lip." Umm, no. I don't write *that* kind of stories! But that was a stupid glitch in a story I had polished until it was turning transparent and threadbare. Any mistakes in here are not through carelessness. Besides, what you see as mistakes could be a difference in opinion on what makes mistakes, or are stylistic decisions.)

I'm not talking about an occasional typo, or a glitch where a word is spelled correctly, it just isn't the word the author wanted. For example, when I worked for a recruitment advertising agency, clients were constantly sending us ad copy asking for mangers -- what they wanted was managers. The computer spell check didn't flag it as a typo because it wasn't. Technically. No, the mistakes I'm talking about are constant inconsistencies, flipping their/there/they're, affect for effect, etc. Lots of them.

Honestly, how can I trust *all* the advice about the writing craft they offer, when they can't handle simple things like sticking with the subject, keeping verb tense consistent, keeping plurals consistent, and using proper grammar? (How many times have I read a famous author saying, "When *Publishers Weekly* interviewed Clarence and I ..."? NO -- "*Publishers Weekly* interviewed Clarence and **me**." You wouldn't say, "They interviewed I," would you? "They interviewed me." [I wish!] So what makes you think that changes when another person is added to the sentence? Grrrrrrrrrrrr!)

Who do we blame? The author, who made the original mistakes? Or can we pass it off on the copy editor or the typesetter, who thought (mistakenly, arrogantly) there were errors and went in and made changes without permission, without checking with someone -- and then didn't make changes consistently throughout? The biggest ones (and they drive me **nuts**!) come from this new fashion of putting punctuation **outside** of quote marks. (I don't care if *Jeopardy* does it that way, it's still sloppy! Alex Trebek is not the arbiter of all intelligentsia!) Honestly, where did that come from? Sure, they use it in some countries in Europe, and my publisher in Australia insists on periods and commas being outside quote marks when I'm referring to *titles of books and records and things like that*, but seriously? Putting exclamation points and question marks outside of quote marks when it's **dialog**? And the copy editor let it go through?

Or an author who is teaching proper grammar and sentence structure says, "try and figure out ..." Excuse me, there is no "try and" there is only "try to." If you "try and do" something, then there are **two** verbs in that sentence, two actions recommended. What are you trying, and what are you doing? No, you are trying **to** do something. Honestly, what is wrong with these people, that they think they can teach me to make **my** writing better when they're making mistakes like that?

Or people putting apostrophes in front of the S when they make something plural? Excuse me, but the apostrophe-S combination meant **possessive**, not plural. (Except in special instances, where a letter stands alone.) No! A thousand times (not time's) **NO**!

Or how about this? "The car full of balloons were flying around the corner." What is flying around the corner? The car (singular), not the balloons (plural). Do I have to diagram the sentence so you know what is acting, and what word the verb applies to? The car is acting, and the balloons filling the car modify the car, so the verb applies to the car, not the balloons. "The car (full of balloons) **was** flying around the corner." And yet I see gaffs like this in articles from (alleged) writing teachers.

It's no wonder the books I edit come to me so full of stupid mistakes -- the examples the public sees every day teach them the wrong way to do it. On TV, in printed ads, on billboards, on the PowerPoint display with lyrics during worship, sermon notes, speeches by public figures (and they have paid speech writers, who *ought* to know better), and what's really horrifying, articles in magazines for writers. Come on, writers -- we're the guardians of language. Do your job!

Do Yourself a Favor: Tips and Quips on the Writing Life
WRITING CONFERENCES -- GO!

I'm surprised when people ask if writing conferences are "worth it." (Granted, some conferences are disappointing, but mostly because they either didn't deliver on what they promised, or the attendees didn't check to see what was offered.)

I'm even more surprised when some people respond to questions about a conference they attended by saying it was a waste of their time because they didn't get anything they wanted or needed. Did they check out the classes and workshops offered, the focus of the conference, the keynote speakers, the writing group sponsoring the conference <u>ahead of time</u>? If you do your homework, you know what you'll be getting. That means unless someone was lying big-time, it *won't* be a waste of your time and money and effort. (If you know the conference isn't offering any workshops that interest you or apply to your needs, then it's on your own head if you go and waste your time and money.)

Of course, you have to be open to learning. You have to be ready to learn. Don't just sit there expecting someone to spoon-feed you.

Yes, conferences are worth it. Even if you know the basics of what the workshops are offering, it's still worth going. Just like it's worth reading books on writing that you've read before: You need to refresh your memory. You need to hear what you already know presented <u>in new ways</u>, learn to see the rules, the guidelines, <u>from a different angle</u>. Sometimes all it takes is a different approach, hearing people talk about how they handle the same blocks and puzzles and decisions, to get that "Ah ha!" moment.

We all need "Ah ha!" moments.

We also need to get together with people who are going through the same struggles of finding inspiration, rough drafting, revising, polishing, marketing, and then promoting. Even though writing is usually a very solitary occupation -- maybe *because* it is so solitary -- we **need** to get together with people who know what we're talking about -- the ones in the trenches with us -- who will nod and pat our hands and say, "I know what you're going through." Because you can only take so much of the "Huh?" looks from people who don't understand.

Find a writer's conference, no matter how small. So what if the next one you can go to is only a day long and doesn't offer a chance to pitch to editors and agents? Go to the ones that offer learning and refreshing and fellowship. That's what we need. Go to the little conferences. The bite taken out of your checkbook won't be that big -- it might not even sting -- but chances are you'll get a lot of the same benefits you would from the big (big as in lost-in-the-crowd, big as in credit card bills, big as in four miles of steps, every day, on your fitness monitor because of all the walking you put in from one end of the campus or hotel to the other) conferences.

- ✓ *Do Yourself A Favor*: Invest your attention and your time in that conference. Open your mouth and talk to people. Don't just go to the conference, sit in the back row, take notes, and leave without making eye contact and learning the names of the people around you.

Go back to the previous paragraph. Re-read what I said about **fellowship**. That means making contact and learning about the people there. Sometimes the best part of some of the conferences I've attended have been the people I've met. You never know when someone you handed the bread basket to, or helped out by digging into that tub of ice up to your elbow for the last bottle of peach tea, will be an editor or agent who will remember you because you were just plain nice to them, saw them as people and not a pen poised over a checkbook.

I heard a story about an RWA conference, where a bunch of "we're all that" writers were quite frankly rude. They must have decided some people there were beneath them, or didn't belong at the conference, or maybe didn't acknowledge that they were indeed "all that." The next day, one of the rude twits walked into an editor appointment, and there at the table was one of those "unworthy" people. The editor, from a big publishing house, remembered this twit. She said something along the lines of, "Don't even bother sitting down."

A bunch of people from my former RWA chapter were hanging around together at a conference set in New Orleans. We had an evening free before the conference got underway, and we went out walking, seeing the sights, getting hot and sweaty and tired. We came back to the hotel and the heroine of this story took off her shoes and walked across the fancy tiled lobby barefoot. We were all just punchy tired, and maybe a little giddy-loud. Our heroine got in an elevator with some strangers and she apologized for being barefoot and ready to fall over. She made everyone in the elevator laugh by relating some of the things we had done. The next day, she walked into her editor appointment, and there at the table was one of the women in the elevator. Our heroine could have died of embarrassment right there. She took a deep breath, spread her arms wide and declared, "I'm baa-aaa-ack!" The editor laughed and they had a great pitch session. Our heroine didn't sell her book, but she made a good impression.

That's the important thing.

- *Do Yourself A Favor*: no matter how much it hurts, make a good impression at writing conferences. You never know who is going to be watching and taking notes. Someone who is a nobody today could be an editor several years down the road, with veto power over your book. And hey, we're writers: it's our job to notice and remember details. Elephants got nothing on us!

Michelle L. Levigne
EVERYBODY NEEDS FRIENDS

Writing is a solitary occupation. We need lots of time, hiding away with our computers, preferably in some place where people can't walk in or plop down in a nearby chair and start talking, and even though they can see we are hard at work, typing away at our computers ... *sigh* ... they expect us to carry on conversations with them or abandon what we're doing to socialize with them.

It's especially irritating when certain people in our lives have this incredible talent -- maybe even an instinct -- for knowing when we are most "in the flow" or struggling the hardest for the right word. That's when they choose to ask questions or start talking about inane things like their shopping list for tomorrow. And they get upset with us when we're angry at being interrupted. Like we don't have the right to be angry when they destroy the flow, when the images we're in the process of putting into words just evaporate, and we have no real hope of recreating them. Gone. Shattered. Shredded.

grrrrrrrrrrrr.......

Did you see *The Man Who Invented Christmas*? About Charles Dickens, writing *A Christmas Carol*. So many of my writing friends said I had to see it, or they wanted to see it, because of all the frustrations he faced, the blocked inspiration, the interruptions, the way he picked up names and details, the way events in his life influenced what he wrote, the interruptions, the battle to get the book published, the interruptions.

Did I say *interruptions* yet? I watched the movie on DVD recently with some non-writers who shall remain nameless, and I held my breath during the scene when Dickens' ne'er-do-well father barges into his office and states yes, he knows Dickens is working hard, he's against a deadline, he knows that no one is allowed into his office while he's working, but he just wanted to tell him something, and borrow a cigar, and several other inane comments. Then when Dickens has reached a slow boil and steam is coming out of his ears, his father smiles and says basically, "Okay, go back to writing. Pick up where you left off." (Jonathan Pryce played his father. Man, I thought I despised his characters in *Something Wicked This Way Comes* and *Tomorrow Never Dies* ...)

Oh, sure, if it's that easy, just "Pick up where you left off," then it's perfectly fiiiiiine to interrupt a writer so hard at work that blood is seeping from her ears and eyes and the tips of her fingers ...

Why is it ten times more frustrating when people who *know* they shouldn't interrupt you do so, and then get *their* feelings hurt because you're angry with them? Like *they* didn't do anything wrong? No, *you're* the one who's wrong for expecting them to put your needs first once every twenty years or so. Oh, no, you are supposed to always put other people first, especially the ones who smile and say, "I know I'm interrupting, but you can get right back to what you're doing even though I've driven the scene you've been struggling to assemble completely out of your head. One scene is as good as another. My need to babble about getting gum out of the hem of my shirt is far more important than a scene for a book you have to turn in to the publisher in one week, and if you miss the deadline you not only have to refund the advance money, but your ten-book contract gets canceled and we'll miss the mortgage payments. My needs will always be more important than yours." *Sniffle.*

(I did post a snark warning elsewhere in this book, didn't I?)

Yeah, during that scene in the movie, I held my breath, wondering if my fellow viewers would pick up on the frustration and pain Dickens was going through, and make the connection a little personal, maybe coming up with the idea that when I'm working, my head is bent over the computer and my fingers are flying on the keyboard and the tapping is loud enough to be heard over my writing music, that maybe, *just maybe,* that's the absolutely wrong time to start a conversation about a TV show I never watched, fifteen years ago.

Yeah, dream on.

- ✓ *Do Yourself A Favor:* find people who think like you and have writing dreams like you. People who will understand and sympathize and offer either a cabin in the mountains to retreat to, or the phone number of someone named Guido, who specializes in "eliminating" troublesome sources of frustration. Bulk discount, anyone?

We need to find some writing friends. Desperately. For our mental health. If not the continued physical well-being of the people who spend more than an hour each day in our company.

People who understand the trials and tribulations we endure. People who want to strangle their loved ones for interrupting, expecting them to drop whatever they're writing, despite the fact they have a deadline. (The same people who say, "Well, if you had a deadline, why didn't you get started on it sooner?" And when responded to with, "You keep interrupting!" they get huffy again.)

Like it's the writer's fault that no one respects their time and the things they value?

Well ... maybe that is partly true. How hard is it to invest in some barbed wire to put across your office door, and make the insulation thick enough to be soundproofing, and turn off the cell phone? Forget about a *Do Not Disturb* sign. The nitwits in your house developed selective illiteracy years ago. "Oh, no, I'm sorry, I did not see the note, in letters three inches tall, taped to the door at eye-level, asking me to pick you up from work because the car is dead because the engine blew a rod because I didn't get the oil changed after you asked me, five times. Why did you walk all that distance in the rain? Suddenly it's my fault you couldn't call me, just because I took your cell phone because I forgot to charge mine? Don't expect me to nursemaid you through this cold. I have important things to do with my day."

Yeah, you need to get out of the house and away from the people who are most precious to you. For your own good. A homicide charge does not look good in the "About the Author" section.

Find a writing group, or at least find a few friends who are also writers. Critique groups are fine, although I've never managed to fit into one. Each writer is different, with different needs and abilities. Some people love critique groups and swear by them. Other people swear *at* them. Some people click immediately. Others click as a prelude to a tirade or a bomb going off. Some people profit from critique groups. I don't. Every critique group I ever joined wanted to put a limit on how many words I could turn in each week. *Excuse me? I'm constantly under deadlines -- I write that many words in a **day**, forget about a week!*

Find people who like and write the same genres that you do. That kinda-sorta ensures they speak, if not the same language as you, then a decipherable dialect. A writing friend was working on a YA historical about two brothers. Her former critique partners wrote category romances. They kept applying romance rules to her story (how can the heroine show up in the first five pages when there is **no heroine**?) and got snippy when she refused to change her story to fit their mold. They kept telling her she was writing her book the wrong way, because she didn't do it *their* way.

- ✓ *Do Yourself A Favor:* Find people who will also be honest with you, even as they're sympathizing or cheering. And denying or indulging in some serious jealousy when you get far ahead of them in attaining your writing dreams.

While it's nice to have a group of friends who pat you on the back and give hugs after every page you turn in, how much good will it do you in the long run if they love everything you write and never point out what you're *not* doing right? At the opposite extreme, avoid the people who are only going to focus on what you're doing wrong. Find a happy medium -- people who see what's good in the story and tell you, and then point out what needs fixing. Preferably, they have enough experience to know *how* to fix it. Preferably, they've listened to you talk about your book, your vision for it, and they know what you're trying to do so they don't try to constantly use a cookie cutter on you. (see previous rant about cookie cutters)

Essentially, you need writing friends who are committed to helping you be the best writer *you* can be. The best version of you -- not a clone of them. Never get tied up with people who try to change your writer's voice. Another writing friend ran afoul of someone who considered herself an expert in everything worth knowing, apparently. This alleged expert reviewed her book and filled it with spoilers. (Spoilers: revealing so much about events and characters and the plot of the book, it's a waste of money and time to buy the book.) Worse: she insisted the book was loaded with "mistakes."

What this self-styled expert considered "mistakes" were differences in voice and style between my friend's way of writing, and what she considered the one-and-only-right-way of writing. She belonged to the ultra-polished writing school, and the so-called "rule" my friend violated was to use the same word more than once in a paragraph -- and better not to use words more than once on a page. For instance, if the heroine was mentioned by name in the first sentence, her name couldn't be used again until the next **page**. Each time thereafter, the author had to find a new word to use to fill in for the heroine. I'm all for being sparing with names, especially in dialog, but this rule can lead to ridiculous extremes.

For example: Becky is the heroine. The next time she moves or speaks or someone looks at her in the scene, she is referred to as "the girl," then "the young lady," then "the eldest daughter of the household," then "the shy sylph," then "the sweet young thing," then "her grandmother's favorite," then "her mother's darling," then "the talented young baker."

Need I go on?

On a side note: Don't go to the other extreme, and use nothing *but* the character's name each time he or she does or says something. Don't slap a name or a tag on every single bit of dialog. Try to make your writing as invisible as possible. Give the readers the benefit of the doubt that yes, they can follow dialog without a name on every single line, and remember who is speaking. Every three or four lines, it's safe to refresh reader's memories. And of course, when a third or a fourth or even a fifth person joins the conversation, then yes, you need to tag the dialog. Especially when the rhythm is broken. Generally, if someone speaks, then a second person speaks, it's assumed that the next line of dialog goes back to the previous person if there's no tag attached to it.

"Said" is pretty invisible. Don't stretch your brain out of shape, trying to come up with a dozen synonyms for it. Only use fancy modifiers if they convey the emotions involved. Snarled, whispered, sighed, snapped, etc.

Another way of avoiding using "said" and tagging the dialog is to have the speaker addressing someone else in the scene. But this has to be a special occasion, or putting special emphasis on what is being said, because if you listen to people speak, they rarely address each other by name in normal conversation -- unless they're trying to get someone's attention, or conveying emotion. Just think back to how much emotion, such as a reprimand or excitement, your mother or your child or your boyfriend can convey in just saying your name. In normal conversation, people don't address each other by name, because they know who they're talking to. Especially if there are only two people in the room or the scene!

Another side note: avoid the "as you know" scenes, where characters tell each other details of their lives the other person in the conversation already knows, or worse yet, events they went through together. It's very obvious that the conversation is there just to bring the reader up to speed. If the information is vital for readers to know, then either just relay it in narrative, or have someone "in the know" relay the information to someone who doesn't know. This has been occasionally referred to as the "dumb puppet scene," where someone who is totally new to the situation asks questions for the sole purpose of giving readers information. As you gain experience, you'll find ways to avoid using the dumb puppet without inflicting an info dump on readers. This is one of those things I consider jalapenos in writing: something that is better off used sparingly, in tiny bits, spaced far apart in the course of the book. Once you start lecturing your readers, you'll lose them.

- ✓ *Do Yourself a Favor*: never, ever, ever, give your readers a reason to close the book and go do something else. Info dumps and "as you know" scenes do just that.

I've seen far too many opening scenes --- and scenes later in the book -- with conversations like this:

"*Francis, how are you?*"

"*Very well, thank you, Delores. And you?*"

"*Oh, Francis, you know how it goes.*"

"*Yes, Delores, I do. And how is your lovely husband, George, and your oldest daughter, Clair, and your second daughter, Evangeline, and your youngest child, Peter?*"

"*Francis, thank you for asking. My husband George ...*"

Get the idea? (Like, really, Delores doesn't know the names of her husband and children, and their birth order, and has to be reminded? What's wrong with, "So, tell me about the family"?)

Don't let people interfere with your voice, your style of writing. If you're a Hemmingway, with a sparse, journalistic style, don't let someone badger you into using so much description the page drips purple ink. If you like being generous with description or action, don't let someone nag you into becoming minimalist just because *they* insist that any kind of description or setting the scene is wrong.

Of course, finding out what works for you, what doesn't work for you, what cramps your style and what gives you hives will take time. Experiment! Like in cooking, you taste test what you're making as you go along, and then you give a sample of the finished product to someone who has the same tastes as you. For goodness' sake, find out what your readers or audience or taste testers like and don't like -- and what they're allergic to. The peanut butter cake you spent all day baking could be delicious, but nobody is going to want to touch it after you ask someone with deathly nut allergies to sample it, and they're rushed to the hospital, swollen and vomiting and struggling to breathe. The same with your writing: figure out who your audience is, and then listen to their feedback.

- ✓ *Do Yourself A Favor:* experiment.
- ✓ *Do Yourself A Favor:* learn something about your readers before you have them read.

You'll all be happier as a result. Trust me.

Okay, rabbit trail ended. Back to the critique or writing group:

If the people you end up joining are an organized group belonging to a professional writing organization, that's fine. Such groups offer connections to and advice and input from the "gatekeepers" -- editors and agents. At the same time, *be careful* of these groups. Their leadership can often insist on forcing you into their specific mold. If you don't do it their way, whether regarding topics, themes, or the kinds of publishers you submit to, they will insist your book isn't a "real" book. Avoid groups that try to make everyone cookies from the same cutter.

I belonged to a writing organization and had to jump ship during the hottest time of the debate over whether e-books were "real" books. The leadership insisted they were there to help us explore our options and grow and make connections and most of all, find our voices and get published. The books we wrote were considered "genre" and "commercial," so of course that meant the "literary" writers and publishers looked down on us and the publishers we sold to. I lost count of the times I would hear sob stories full of righteous indignation, how someone would be having a wonderful conversation about writing with another writer, until the other author learned this writer wrote genre. The response was always along the lines of, "When are you going to write a *real* book?" And when this story of emotional abuse and scorn was related, the battle cry would rise up, declaring, "No one has the right to tell you your book is not a real book!"

Then along came e-books, and the same people who suffered "abuse" from "literary" writers turned to e-published authors and said, "When are you going to write a *real* book?" Like, the difference between electrons and processed wood pulp determined "reality"?

This attitude was all over the writing industry. People I knew in EPIC (an electronic publishing organization) were being invited to speak about writing and fawned on because they had twenty or more titles, and making enough money from sales to live on their writing income. Then they were dis-invited and publicly scorned, when the conference organizers and leadership of their particular writing organization made the "disappointing" discovery that those were all e-books. Meaning they weren't "real" books.

You want to know irony? The same professional writing organization I left made a swift turnaround only a year or so later, and was suddenly, "Rah, rah! E-books are going to save our careers! Hurrah for e-books!"

In case you've been drinking the Kool-Aid, a certain big-name book retailer did NOT invent e-books. Dozens of small presses were the pioneers, and fought in the trenches and took abuse from publishers, editors, and writers organizations for years. They sold books on disks, in HTML and PDF and other document formats. People read them on computers and PDAs long before dedicated readers and tablets and cellphones and .mobi and .ePub came along. Don't believe the big-name publishers who broadly hint that they invented e-books. They only made them acceptable and accessible after the "little guys" did all the hard work.

Bitter? Moi?

Be prepared to run into people along your writing journey who will make the arbitrary decision, based on *their* personal tastes and values and experience, that *your* book doesn't qualify as real. Doesn't have value. Will never sell. You gotta find your audience, you gotta find your readers, you gotta find the people who like the same things you like, and **write for them.**

We all gotta have friends. Now, more than ever.

Find a group of people who feed you, support you, kiss your boo-boos, and then shove you out of the nest to try again. (Need I say here that you should be prepared to return the favor?) People who believe you can produce masterpieces, and then won't cut you any slack until you do so. They demand your best. They love you. They understand your stories and your way of looking at the world, but don't let you get away with anything. These are friends who, while they might get jealous sometimes, still help you to grow as a writer.

You can't do it alone, even if you spend ninety percent of your time in solitary confinement.

Do Yourself a Favor: Tips and Quips on the Writing Life

THE RIGHT WORD VS. THE ALMOST-RIGHT WORD

Homonyms: sound-alike words. Using *perspective* when you mean *prospective*. Using *their* when you mean *there*. *It's* for *its*. *Adapt* for *adopt*.

Some people may say, "Well, it's close enough to what you mean, people can figure it out, so why does it matter to get the right word?"

It Matters.

To misquote Mark Twain: The difference between the right word and the almost-right word is the difference between lightning and a lightning bug. Or maybe it was fire and firefly. There was an insect there somewhere. (Wouldn't you like to know what the actual quote was? Or if it was even said by Mark Twain? Aren't you kind of ticked that I didn't take the time to look it up to be sure? Kind of like those people who want to be writers but won't take the time to learn and make sure they got it right ... Are you learning, Grasshopper?)

If you want to be a writer, you have to get it right.

That means the details. That means the mechanics.

If *you* don't care about the details, why should your readers care about the story you want to tell? If you have a story to tell, and you're going to spend the time getting the rest of it "right," why wouldn't you make the effort to use the right words?

If you're going to take the time to weave together the story so it makes sense, so it catches and holds the reader's attention, so the reader cares about the characters, the conflict, the danger, the goals, the tension -- why would you get sloppy (read: lazy) when it comes to the actual words and the meanings of the words you use to tell the story?

It makes me want to pull out my hair, to read stories where the words are so badly chosen, so very wrong for what I know the writer means, that it distracts me from the story. You don't want to frustrate the reader, to the point of putting down the book and not picking it up again, do you? (I just started editing a book where the author wrote, talking directly to the readers, "I no, I no, I'm preaching to the chore ..." AARRGGHH!)

So learn the difference between *affect* and *effect* -- between *insure*, *assure* and *ensure* -- *adapt* and *adopt* -- *perspective* and *prospective* -- *their*, *they're*, and *there* -- *its* and *it's* -- *or* and *oar* -- *are*, *our*, and *hour* -- *fare* and *fair* -- even *aide* and *aid* -- on and on. Learn what the words mean, and use them correctly!

Michelle L. Levigne

WORDS, WORDS, WORDS

This is just basically a list of more homonyms that I see switched and used interchangeably (and what's really sad, intended to mean the same thing in the same sentence or paragraph):

Hurdle and hurtle -- do you know the difference? One is an obstacle, one is a verb employed when going over the other.

Shudder and shutter -- one is a verb, the other is a noun

Prophecy and prophesy -- no, they don't mean the same thing, they aren't even pronounced the same. One's a noun, one's a verb.

Alter and altar

Trials and trails

Accept and except

Bought and brought

Allude and elude

Then and than -- one indicates a sequence of events, the other indicates comparison

Won't and want -- seriously! I've seen more instances of people writing "I won't an extra piece of pie, " or "He want be ready on time." (*banging head on wall* Or maybe we need to be slapping some lazy teachers upside the head?)

Manager and manger

Viscous and vicious (although come to think of it, if you fall into something viscous, that's a pretty vicious reaction ...)

Patients and patience -- one is a group of people in need of medical care, and the other is a quality

Barley and barely and bearly (the last isn't really a word, but people still use it)

(While we're here: Bare and bear)

Temporal and temporary -- one refers to elements of time, while the other refers to something lasting only a short period of time, no staying power.

Shinning and shining -- shinning refers to climbing, but people insisting on applying it to lights. Lights shine, they do not shin and do not climb, as far as I know ...

Hoping and hopping -- I think the same people who want to have double consonants when they talk about lights do the same thing with hope. Do not ask me why. One is done in the head or heart, the other is the action of going up and down in rapid succession.

Apart and a part -- one is the opposite of the other, if you think about it. If you are *apart*, you are not *a part* of the group. Right? So don't use them interchangeably!

Breathe/breathes and breath/breaths -- the first is a verb, the second is what you are controlling when you do the first.

Choose and chose -- the first is present tense of the second, which is past tense of the action done with the first.

Sense and since and scents and cents -- why people use these interchangeably, I do not know, except maybe they're lazy and they write by the "What does it sound like?" method -- and ignore the spell checker and grammar checker built into their word processing program. Again, I ask, WHY?

Advise and advice -- this is like prophesy and prophecy, one is the verb of when you dispense the other.

Vise and vice -- one is a construction tool and the other is a bad habit or a sin. Granted, some dictionaries have given in and allow one to stand for both, but please ... we're better than that, aren't we?

Teeth and teethe -- again, noun and verb that uses the noun, or more appropriately, the verb in action when you are gaining the noun.

Vertebrate and vertebra -- You are not the one if you do not have a few of the other.

Taut and taunt -- I have a writing friend who keeps doing this in the stories she has me edit. "His taunt muscles." Huh? Like ... his muscles were mocking someone?

Passed and past -- one is past tense of a verb, and the other is an element of time

Posses and possess

Decrease and decease.

Rode and road -- he rode down the road ....

Whole and hole -- if it has a hole, it is not whole.

Too many people nowadays are writing "use" when they need "used" because it is past tense, meaning "formerly," as in, "He used to understand." "She used to have a vase just like that." And yet I see "use" far too often, and from people who should know better, with three, five, a dozen books under their belts. Are they just getting lazy, or do they have editors who don't slap them upside the head for dropping the highly valuable and functional "d" from the word?

Then there are the people who are writing what they THINK they hear-- kind of like the people who sing along with songs they've learned off the radio. When you confront them with the lyrics from the liner notes off the album, they either get really embarrassed, or they get nasty and accuse you of lying. All it takes is a check of the liner notes, or an online search, and yet they act like they are the victims. No, they're too busy or lazy to check. How hard is it to get on the Internet and search the lyrics of a song? (sorry, yet another tangent)

When I was proofreading for a legal publishing company, I got this mistake often from lawyers -- *allegedly*, highly educated people: Buy in large.

Umm, no, the proper wording is **By And Large**. (Unless of course you're referring to the corporation that destroyed Earth's ecology in the movie *WALL-E*.)

Another "duh!" I've been seeing more and more (really should research these people and see if they went to the same school and had the same teacher ...):

"Working progress" instead of "work in progress."

Big difference, you think?

- ✓ *Do Yourself A Favor*: learn to use the tools before you try to create something splendiferous, okay?

To continue:

Despite its common usage, alright is not all right.

I'm totally with Professor Strunk, E.B. White's mentor: avoid wordiness. When one word will do, why use three, or four, or ten?

Avoid wordiness and extraneous, redundant words. I catch a lot of people say things like, "He shrugged his shoulders," or "He nodded his head," or "He saw with his eyes," or "He smelled it with his nose." Excuse me, but it's kind of understood that when you nod, it's done with your head. What else can you shrug but your shoulders? How else do you see except with your eyes? (Yes, the blind see with their fingers, but it's not common, know what I mean?) A really aggravating thing I see in books, and hear on the radio and during sports coverage and basically everywhere: *I thought to myself*. Excuse me, but unless you're telepathic, who else are you going to think to, who else will hear your thoughts, other than yourself? So keep it simple, and avoid wordiness:

I thought.

I shrugged.

I nodded.

I saw.

I smelled.

More wordiness? How about "In order to"? Why not keep it simple and simply say, "to"?

"He got up early in order to have time to cook breakfast for his children."

"He got up early to have time to cook breakfast for his children."

Two fewer words, and there's no change in the meaning.

Simplify. Cut down on wordiness and redundancies and things that are simply understood and don't need to be pointed out, okay?

Then there's what I call Impossible Body Parts Movements.
His eyes traveled the room.
No, his eyes did not pop out of his head and roll across the floor and up the walls.
*His **gaze** traveled the room.*
When you write about different parts of your body doing things -- THINK. Did they *really* do that?

I recently edited a book where there were some semi-fight scenes. In one, the suspected terrorist threw his leg at the Border Patrol agent who was tailing him. (Giggle-snort. Or on second thought, eww, gross.) Umm ... no. He did not disengage his leg and fling it at her like a spear. He kicked at her. His leg stayed attached to his body.

He flung his hands up in the air. Umm ... no. He did not detach his hands and toss them up like a graduate would toss his mortarboard. He snapped his arms up in the air and waved his hands. Or something along those lines.

Or the writing friend I edit says things like, "He turned his neck." What about his head, *attached* to his neck?

- ✓ *Do Yourself A Favor*: Think, really think -- draw a diagram, use dolls if that helps -- act out what exactly your characters are doing when you say their legs and hands and tongues and jaws (really? His jaw hit the ground? It fell off his face? Or did he go down on his knees?) and eyes and ears are acting *separately* from the rest of their bodies.

His ears swiveled. Really? They turned independently of his head like radar dishes? *His face turned to the enemy.* What about the rest of his head? *His tongue fell out of his mouth.* And then he put it back in his mouth after it was on the floor? Yuck.

(Seems to me something is physically wrong if his tongue detached from his body. Like something is rotten. I wouldn't put a piece of half-dead meat in my mouth, even if it started there. Just ... disgusting. Granted, there was this weirdo character in the first season of *Angel* who could send different parts of his body flying around, but ... you aren't writing that kind of semi-horror, supernatural story, are you?)

Basic rule to follow: if that body part has to detach from the character's body to do what you want it to do ... ain't gonna happen! (Unless it's a spin-off of *The Walking Dead*. Maybe *Crawling Body Parts*?)

Then there's the rule that everyone breaks at some time or another... attaching actions or modifiers to the dialog that have no impact whatsoever on the words.

"Sure," he nodded.

"How can you say that?" she fainted.
"You flatter me," he bowed.
Etc., etc., ad nauseum.

- ✓ *Do Yourself A Favor*: If it doesn't affect how the words are said, such as the tone of voice, don't attach it to the attribution or modifier of the dialog and make it part of the same sentence.

What do I mean by that?
Ralph walked into the room, "That's awful." (And the snarky examples above.)

Umm, walking into the room does not affect *how* the words were said. The physical action is separate from the words.

You can't walk your words, blink your words, swing your words, dunk your words, wave your words, smile your words, glare your words, etc. Get the picture?

Some modifiers and attributions that people try to get away with … well, it's tricky.

"I can't believe that," he laughed.

Have you ever tried to laugh and talk at the same time? Try it -- right now. Laugh and talk at the same time. Can anyone understand you?

Then don't make your characters laugh while they're talking -- unless, of course, they're laughing so hard what they're trying to say is unintelligible. (Side note: spoken words aren't illegible, because illegible relates to writing not to understanding or hearing clearly.)

- ✓ *Do Yourself A Favor*: really think about the words you're attaching to dialog, or using as modifiers, okay?

You can sigh your words, shout, roar, whimper, whisper. Other modifiers are iffy, and it would be better if it was an extra tag at the end.
"You can't do that." His voice crackled as he said it.

Make sense? If the action or modifier does not affect the voice and how the words are spoken, it's just safer, neater, and makes more sense if they're in a separate sentence.

However … yeah, there's always an exception … you can insert action in the middle of speaking.

"Howard's never going to accept," he said, standing and crossing the room to hand George the papers, "that you and I are working together."

If you must have action attached to the words, because the character is speaking and acting at the same time, then just use the handy and clearly understood "as" or "while" or "during." And of course, add that the person SAID, while performing the action.

Do Yourself a Favor: Tips and Quips on the Writing Life

"*You're going about this all wrong,*" she said, as she picked up the neglected wire whisk, and took over mixing the cake batter. NOT: "*You're going about this all wrong,*" picking up the wire whisk, to take over mixing the cake batter.

Clear enough?

Next item on my rant list: Britishisms

I'm not talking about dialect -- although my feelings about weird spelling to recreate dialect/pronunciations, or give an idea of an accent is the same as my feelings about back story: treat dialect and weird spellings like jalapenos. Use them lightly, for seasoning. Don't let them overwhelm the rest of the story.

(Don't even get me started on this unspoken rule that when you go to a fantasy world, everybody must speak with a British accent. Even if it's retelling mythology, set in Greece or Egypt or Africa, everybody speaks with a British accent. I'm not griping about movies based on books written by British authors, so don't accuse me of that. I'm talking about the accents that don't make sense! Did anyone ever wonder why Jean Luc Picard, who is *French*, spoke with a British accent? Come on, Patrick Stewart is a good enough actor, he could have come up with a French accent, but nooooo, the producers never asked him for it. Note: If my fantasy books are ever turned into movies, ***no one is allowed to speak with a British accent!***)

What I mean by Britishisms is using British spelling in a book set in America, where the main characters are Americans.

Writing Saviour instead of the American Savior
Behaviour instead of Behavior
Flavour instead of Flavor
Favour instead of Favor
Colour instead of Color
Get the idea? (Basically extra letters)

It's one thing to use the British spelling when you're quoting from books and articles and the King James version of the Bible -- *do not change the spelling of the source document*. But don't let that change the proper spelling of those words in the rest of the book. Go to the Language selection controls in your word processing program and make sure it's set for English: United States. Then, every time you get that red squiggle underneath a word, when you think the word is spelled right, check the built-in dictionary. The spell check function is flagging you that even if the word looks right, it's wrong.

If you want your book written full of Britishisms, then go ahead, set the language for British English -- but be aware that unless the publisher is in the UK, house style will probably dictate that you get rid of the Britishisms. Your editor will not appreciate having to work around it.

So just don't, okay?

Last item before we move on to something else to grumble about: Capitalization.

Be consistent. Proper names and titles are capitalized. Labels are not.

To illustrate:

I was talking to Pastor Wilson yesterday

Vs.

I was talking to our pastor yesterday.

See the difference? When "pastor" is part of a name, it's capped -- when it's a label or descriptor, it's not.

But just to make things complicated, using pastor as a name, it's capped.

"Hi, Pastor, what's up?"

Make sense?

So:

The president of the homeowner's association vs. President Tucker

The captain of the starship vs. Captain Kirk

The general vs. General Patton

Then there's the really frustrating tendency of people who insist on capitalizing qualities:

When Love is in your heart, you must hold to what you know is Truth and keep your Faith strong.

No! Unless those qualities are the names of people, or maybe with a stretch, anthropomorphic characters in a book ... just don't.

Like too many jalapenos, capitalizing everything will make the capitals lose their effectiveness.

The same with **boldfacing** and *italicizing* and <u>underlining</u>. Do it sparingly, otherwise it all melts together into a mess that the eye skims right over, and nothing sinks into the brain.

Rant over.

For now ... (mwah hah hah...)

PUNCTUATION CRIMES

Repeat after me: Quote marks come in pairs. (Generally. We won't go into the rules for handling quotes that go on for several paragraphs.)

I don't know what's wrong with the lessons in English classes the last twenty years. When I was in Senior English, five grammar mistakes meant an automatic "F" in our bi-weekly essays. (Thank you, Miss Hazlett. We groaned, but we loved you.)

"Grammar mistakes" also meant spelling and punctuation mistakes. It was just shorter and neater to say two words than a half-dozen, y'know?

The punctuation mistakes I see now dealing with quote marks, I just have to shake my head.

I've seen a single quote -- better known as an apostrophe -- start a line of dialog, to be closed by a double quote. Or the inverse -- a double quote mark starts the line of dialog, and an apostrophe ends it. Or no quote marks at all at the end of the line of dialog. Or nothing at the start of the dialog but quote marks at the end. I'd blame it on simple sloppiness, but when the punctuation is that way through the **whole book** ... consistently wrong.

Quote marks come in pairs -- and quote marks are double quotes, front and back. If you start a quotation or dialog with quote marks, you must mark the end of the quote, or the line of dialog, with quote marks. No exceptions. (UNLESS the house style for your publisher is to use single quote marks to indicate dialog. It all depends on your editor and publisher. And again, your editor might be lenient if you're consistent, and not just sloppy and slapdash.)

Then there's the "fun" of untangling quote marks when you're quoting someone else's written or spoken words within dialog or within quoted material. The simple explanation is that you alternate single quotes and double quotes, to give visual clues of what's being quoted.

For example:

"I'm leaving on Friday," John said.

Patty said, "I heard John say, 'I'm leaving Friday.' So that means we have to have the meeting tomorrow."

Joe reported to the rest of the office, "Patty said, 'I heard John say, "I'm leaving Friday."' But we can't have the meeting tomorrow because we're all tied up in that seminar."

Does that help at all?

It gets even more "fun" (yes, this is what is known as reverse quotes, because putting words in quote marks indicates sarcasm and the opposite meaning of the word.) when you're quoting something that has quote marks within it already. The common practice is to simply put quote marks around the material you're quoting ... and then either through ignorance or laziness or not seeing the quote marks in the material, you don't change the quotation marks within the quoted material. (Man, I'm getting sick of saying quotes and quotations and quoted, aren't you sick of seeing it? Hold on -- the misery is almost over.)

You **must** change the quote marks. This is the only instance when it is technically permitted to make changes to the material you are quoting. For instance, when quoting Bible verses or a passage from a text that has dialog or quoted material within it. Change those double quotes to single quotes if you believe you must put quote marks around the material you are quoting.

My feeling is: Put Bible verses in italics rather than quote marks -- or when quoting more than two lines of material, indent from both sides. Then you don't have to fuss with changing the punctuation. Especially if you're copying and pasting from an electronic text, rather than typing everything in. Keep it simple!

✓ *Do Yourself A Favor*: keep it simple whenever you can.

Semi-colons:
Never.
On pain of death.
Use semi-colons as commas.

Just keep in mind that semi-colons are used to either *connect items in a list*, or they are used to *connect two phrases that could stand on their own* if they were separated.

Example:
Use #1 -- *Here's what you need to bring for the conference: office casual clothes for appointments; a wrap for when the air-conditioning gets to be too much; notepads and pens for taking notes; power cords for your electronics; highlighters and colored pencils for two creativity exercises; one-sheets and sample chapters for the books you want to pitch.*

Use #2 -- *Five days into the training exercise, Cmdr. Kreepo demonstrated just how he earned the moniker; no one who took his classes ever came back for refresher courses.*

Example of how NOT to use semi-colons:
Joan looked out across the playing field; wondering where the infamous "pit" lay among the grass; a week overdue for cutting; and hiding evidence of five solid days of rainfall; and promising a mud-bath for all the players.

So don't use them as commas, okay?

Now we come to parentheses and brackets. When to use them, and when not to use them?

Sometimes the parentheses don't make sense, but how can you know? Here's a trick I learned to use, to determine if words should be in parentheses or not:

First of all, consider them as "asides," such as when a character on stage or in a movie turns away from the other characters and addresses the audience or the camera.

Then, consider everything inside the parentheses or brackets as **invisible words.**

If the sentence doesn't make sense with those parenthetical or bracketed words taken out, then those words most certainly should not be in parentheses or brackets to begin with.

The same can be said for words set off by em-dashes. Double hyphens, for those like me who didn't know the name for a long time, we just used them. Em-dashes are like parentheses: the words inside them are considered invisible. Apply the same test to the words inside the em-dashes, and if the sentence doesn't make sense with those words removed, then remove the em-dashes and rewrite the sentence to use those words.

- ✓ *Do Yourself A Favor:* rewrite the sentence to put the em-dashed or parenthetical words elsewhere, maybe even in a different sentence. Less mental untangling for your readers. Plus, just think about what trouble you're making for a narrator, if your book ever gets turned into an audio book. How exactly do you narrate parentheticals and em-dashes?

Another punctuation "crime" that really bothers me, making me wonder about the quality of education in modern English classes: *Who decided that plurals need to have an apostrophe between the word and the S? Find that person and slap him around until he repents.*

The apostrophe-S combination is for possessive, not plurals.

John's house = the house belonging to John. It doesn't mean a house named after two or more people named John.

To expand on that: the apostrophe-S combination is for singular possessive: John Miller's house.

If you want plural possessive, you switch the order around to S-apostrophe.

The Millers' house = the house belonging to several people named Miller.

Kind of sad that I have to point this out, but considering how many books I've edited that commit this crime consistently, yeah, it has to be said.

Here's another semi-tricky one: when the name ends with s, usually you slap the apostrophe on the end unless -- unless! -- you pronounce the extra s.

For example: John Jones' house

The Joneses' house.

But don't add that extra syllable/s to Jesus. It's just ... wrong ... to say Jesuses. And it looks weird, too. So just make it possessive with the apostrophe, no extra S.

Jesus' words. Not Jesus's.

Make sense?

Do Yourself a Favor: Tips and Quips on the Writing Life
SENTENCE STRUCTURE RANT

✓ *Do Yourself A Favor*: Pay attention to sequences.

What do I mean by sequences? Essentially, separating actions from the people or things acting or being acted on, or putting too much distance between modifiers and the things they modify.

If you put too much distance between object/subject and the action, you can imply things you didn't intend. Yes, readers will understand what you meant, if they take a few seconds more to think, but why do you want to make them stop and look at the sentence and pull their minds out of the flow of the story to figure out what you really meant? Every break in the flow, every instance where they pull out and analyze, is a chance for readers to put down the book and walk away. Give them an excuse to walk away enough times, and they'll never come back to the book. Irritate them enough times, and they'll tell other people what an irritating, uneven, hard-to-follow writer you are. I don't care if some people say that any publicity is good publicity, because it puts your name in people's minds. Negative publicity is still negative publicity.

Here's what I mean by separating object/subject from the actions and modifiers: *She saw a little old man standing next to a red house with a beard wearing a green coat.*

On first glance, will someone get the impression that the house has a beard, and the beard is wearing a green coat? A little bit of proper attention to sequences will lead to a clearer, more sensible word picture: *She saw a little old bearded man, wearing a green coat, standing next to a red house.*

Then the other kind of sequence that gives me fits sometimes: Prepositional phrases. Not the phrases themselves, but the misapplication of the phrases. The general rule to keep in mind is that the first subject AFTER a prepositional phrase that does not name the subject IS the subject of that phrase.

Here's one I've seen several times in different books I've edited. Enough times, in different forms, to really stick in my head: *After wandering lost forty years in the desert, God spoke to the children of Israel.*

Umm ... God was not lost and wandering! *After the children of Israel wandered forty years in the desert, God spoke to them.*

Here's one that someone did to me. They thought they were "helping" by rewriting the back cover blurb of one of my books, but it made no sense, and I was heartily embarrassed: *Wearing a new name and a beard after twelve years, Raine didn't recognize him.*

Umm, no, Raine did not have a beard! The proper phrasing should have been: *Twelve years later, Raine didn't recognize him with a beard and a*

new name.
>Need I say more?

Do Yourself a Favor: Tips and Quips on the Writing Life

REALMIES RULE!

While rough drafting this book, I posed a question along these lines on the Realm Makers Consortium Facebook page:
What words do you see constantly being mis-used, or what grammar mistakes drive you crazy?
These are the people who responded over the course of just two days, and these are their responses in their own words. So see, it's not just me being nitpicky and splitting enough hairs to make Vidal Sasoon swoon!
Thanks all of you, for speaking up!
Kendra Elise Ardnek; Grace Bridges; Heidi Lyn Burke; Sherry Kaye Chamblee; Jessica Cordell; Serena Dawson; Annie Downer; Megan Edlin; Jessica Fry; Rachel Kimberly Hastings; Sara James; Jenelle Leanne; Erika Mathews; Emily Norwood; Jennifer Rempel; Lauren Salisbury; Daphne Self; Kristen Stieffel; Cindy Taylor; Elizabeth West.

Word switches:
Straight/Strait
Lightening/Lightning
Shone/Shown
Than/Then
Converse/Conversate (That's not even a word!)
Lay/Lie
Rise/Raise (Anybody else irritated by the Jeremy Camp song that says, "the power that ROSE Jesus from the dead"? No, YOU rose, but you RAISED someone else... DUH! Them songwriter-type guys down in Nashville otter find themselves an English-type teacher person to teach them some proper-type grammar stuff, y'know?)
Sit/Set
Hoard/Horde
There/Their/They're
Whether/Weather
Your/You're
Bored/Board.
Taught/Taut
Peek/Peak/Piqued.
Preventative/Preventive
Imminent/Eminent/Immanent
Taut/Taunt

Word switches with explanations/tricks for keeping them correct:
The misuse/incorrect belief that loath/loathe and breath/breathe are

interchangeable is one that drives me nuts. I just remember that the "e" on the end helps the "th" sound a bit harder, and that helps me keep track of which is which.

Imminent and eminent! My tip: an alliterative device -- I always think if imminent and impending going hand in hand. "The imminent impending doom was upon us." Whereas eminent goes with excellency, "His Excellency was the most eminent king of all the land."

I learned a great trick for effect and affect: Effect is the noun like sound Effects, and Affect is the verb and is an Action

Similarly grey and gray (if one cares about being precise, and I violate this one all the time because I prefer grey for mysterious things rather than gray) is grEy is from England and grAy is from America.

Pour/Pore -- I actually learned "pore over" is correct not "pour over" when referring to someone reading a book after I already had like three books out.

Bias/biased. People forget the -ed all the time.

Forward and foreword!!! Also, secondarily, the difference between a foreword and an introduction.

Grammar Rants:

"Try AND" drives me up a wall. I get told it's an idiomatic expression now and to just accept it, but ... no. No, I won't. LOL. You're not saying that you're doing two actions, so you don't need "and." I'm not sure why that's hard. You are trying to do ONE thing. You wouldn't say, "I hope and come" if you meant "I hope to come," so why say "I will try and come"?

"May" as past tense when it should be "might."

Using "of" as a helping verb. "I should of done that." Makes me shudder just to type it.

Saying "beside of him." There is no "of" with "beside"!

"Try and" drives me nuts! I teach college English, and the one that gets me is when my students write, "could of" instead of "could've." O.O

And writing "could care less" instead of "couldn't care less." If you could care less, you care.

I realize that usage is shifting on these, but I feel the traditional distinctions between gantlet (ordeal) and gauntlet (glove) and between stanch (stop) and staunch (stalwart) are worth upholding.

Just plain bad, as in wrong punctuation, etc.:

"Orientate" is one that bugs me!

Ya'll instead of y'all

For that matter, any word with a possessive apostrophe. Seems like half the time the apostrophe isn't supposed to be there, and the other half of the time it's misplaced.

Anyways!

I do think that slang terms and casual or dialectal grammar forms are perfectly acceptable in dialog. After all, that's how people talk. Not okay in narrative, though! The author should know better

"At about" is my uber-pet peeve. Someone cannot be "at" and "about" at the same time.

Don't forget the old its/it's confusion. And a few more I've seen: taut/taunt, set/sat, further/farther, seen/saw, bred/bread, ect instead of etc.

The "Might could" discussion just took off...

"Might could," as in "It might could rain." Pick one and stick with it, if you please, there's a good chap.

"Might could" is Southern US dialect. Totally appropriate for a Southern character. But if it's the author's native dialect slipping into the dialog of a Northern character, then it would need to be replaced with something more appropriate.

My brain turns the grammar off for dialog most of the time, and I live in the south so I hear it all the time. It's just...something about 'might could'...it makes absolutely no sense how it's a thing. XD

Again, my thanks to the amazing Realmies!

Michelle L. Levigne

THERE'S RICH, AND THEN THERE ARE RICHES

Let's just get this out in the open here at the beginning: **Don't expect to get rich doing this.**

If you set out on the writing journey with the belief that you'll slap a commercially topical book into the computer, get someone to whip up a snazzy cover, then shove it out there and people will just automatically pick it up and think it's the greatest thing and you'll be rich in time to buy your mother a new house for Christmas ... don't.

How many of us are marketing geniuses AND writers? Because that's what it's going to take to get your book the kind of exposure and support to sell in the kinds of numbers you need to become rich. (After taxes.)

Yes, there are exceptions. Most of them come from unusual circumstances, such as notoriety, of the good and bad varieties. Someone writes a book so controversial that large, vocal groups vilify the subject or the author or both, or someone writes a book that gets an enthusiastic endorsement from a public figure.

Yes, some people just have that knack for promotion and a gift for writing at the same time. The kind of people you don't know whether you should admire them or hire Guido to eliminate them from your rising frustration reservoir. Know what I mean?

For the most part, though, no, we writers are not marketing geniuses. We don't have the time or the money or the creative energy to spend on both writing and marketing. There's only so much time and so much creative energy and so much money, and we have to choose where and how and when and why to spend those limited resources.

So **have fun** with your writing. Follow your dreams, follow your heart, instead of your bank account. Unless your heart is in your bank account. Then I've got no advice for you.

For those who do have the money to hire people to handle the icky chores of promotion and being marketing creative, show some restraint and respect for your fellow writers, and don't brag or mock or criticize those who don't or can't. Either keep quiet, or reach out and help.

Remember: the people you pass on the way up are the same people you will pass on the way down. It'll be up to them if your trip down is nice, and maybe if someone reaches out a hand to catch you on the way down. So don't step on people and kick them in the ribs or poke them in the eyes on the way up. Make sense?

Many people have riches that have nothing to do with being rich.

- ✓ *Do Yourself A Favor:* invest in the things that matter, and value the things that don't depend on bank accounts and sales figures.

THE WRITING PHASE:

Do Yourself a Favor: Tips and Quips on the Writing Life

YOU'RE THE DIRECTOR

One of the first books on screenwriting I read (back in college, I wrote my first screenplay longhand, on notebook paper in a three-ring binder) told me to never put down any stage directions unless those directions were absolutely vital to the movement of the story. Things like character development or inserting details necessary to the plot. Such as: "Jake picks up the talisman and puts it in his pocket." And then later, "The demon appears, streamers of evil magic shoot out his fingers and yank Jake through the wall from the next room, as the talisman glows red-hot in his pocket." Kind of vital to the action and the story progression, ya think?

Why? It is the director's prerogative to decide what the characters/actors do, how they react, and sometimes even put the thoughts and emotions in their heads, affecting how they deliver their lines, how they react to each other, and all the "side business" that they attend to when the camera is focusing on someone else. Essentially, they are living their own characters' lives while the story follows someone else.

When writing a book, you are turning your mental screenplay into a novel, so now **you** are the **director. You** have the power. **You** know what your characters are thinking, why they have to pick up the gun on page 40 so they have the gun to shoot the terrorist or be caught with it and arrested for carrying a concealed weapon on page 100.

Do you know what your characters are thinking, why they react to the sight of cornbread dripping with maple syrup as if it reminds them of the greatest tragedy of their lives? (You need to handle those insights and flashbacks delicately.) Do you know what brought a secondary character into town in time to trigger a bar fight that results in the hero being shot so he's in the hospital when his ex-girlfriend -- who didn't tell him she was pregnant -- is rushed to the hospital to give birth?

You better know -- **You** are the **director**! *(And because audiences, by and large, hate "lucky" coincidences. I'm willing to bet Deus ex Machina endings weren't that popular even in ancient Greek plays. Didn't the Greek gods have better things to do than untangle stupid Humans' lives? It's just a sign/symptom of BAD writing.)*

While some directors are such geniuses that they can just wing it, a lot of directors are geniuses because they plan ahead. They think about each character and scene, and create background. They know the histories, reasons, feelings, what chemical reactions will create the bomb blast they need in the climax scene, and how the hero can defuse the bomb without any training. More important, they know how to insert that information early in the movie, but downplayed so it isn't a red flag, so the audience doesn't say, "Yeah, right, like **that's** believable?" when the hero saves the day. Or what's worse, "Yeah, I saw that coming from a mile away." What writers want is for readers to say at the end of the book, "That makes so much sense, but even though all the clues were there, I did not see that coming. What a great story!"

You need to know these things. You need to plan ahead -- whether you're a plotter or pantser, you need to plan, just in different ways and intensities to suit your style. You need to have conversations with your characters and get to know them. Whatever it takes. One author said in a workshop that she sits down and has coffee with her characters. She knows them well enough to know who will want plain black coffee and who will want a caramel mocha frappe with extra whipped cream. That is the point when you're ready to be the director and move your characters around so the rest of the world thinks you're a genius.

You are the director. Get ready to direct. It's gonna be a great movie -- whether it's on a wide screen or inside your reader's head.

SHOW -- DON'T TELL -- THROUGH SCREENWRITING

Have you heard "Show, Don't Tell" so many times you want to scream?

Especially if you can't quite get the hang of showing what's going on in your characters' heads without simply saying (telling) what they're feeling, as in "Fred was furious"?

- ✓ *Do Yourself A Favor*: Experiment. Play with other forms. In this instance, write a screenplay.

It's not really that hard. There are lots of places where you can get samples of screenplays to see the format. (Not that important, unless you decide you like the technique so much you want to try to write to sell ... which ain't that easy! First rule is to always understand the formats, the mechanics, the rules for whatever genre or form of literature you are working in, like a cook needs to understand the tools and ingredients she uses.)

To write a screenplay, you need directions, you need minimal setting descriptions, and you need dialog. That's it. No interior dialog, no fear of info-dumps that irritate readers. The only way to share information with the audience is through dialog, or action.

Doing this will train you and help you develop a habit that will, in the end, solve a problem many newer writers have: Setting the stage. They forget to say **where** a scene takes place. All they give you is dialog, until suddenly a character walks across the room, revealing they're indoors, and picks up a pan or a letter opener or a file or a pillow, giving some small clue where they are. Or worse, two people are talking, and suddenly a third person joins the conversation, and there was no indication whatsoever a third person was there. When did he arrive? How many other people are there? Or worse, squared, a conversation has been going on for a whole page now, with no names attached to the dialog, so readers have no idea who is talking, or how many people are involved in the conversation. Or suddenly it starts raining -- no indication of the weather. Etc., etc., *ad infinitum, ad nauseum*.

- ✓ *Do Yourself A Favor*: Make a big sign with bright colors to catch your attention, and hang it over your computer or somewhere you will see it every time you sit down to write. A sign that says: SET THE STAGE! Never make your characters act on a blank stage -- or naked!

A standard screenplay will establish time of day (Day, Night, Noon, Dawn, etc.), if it is an exterior or interior scene, and the location, all in the first line. Then right under this line will be a paragraph or two that set the stage -- who is there, what it looks like. "Fred and Lisa walk through the door into an office that has been trashed."

A screenplay will **not** tell you, "Lisa looks around in horror, remembering how she used to come here with her father as a child and learned ..." whatever. A screenplay will say, essentially, "Lisa reacts." Then, it will give dialog to reveal what she is thinking/feeling:

LISA: *This is awful! I can't believe what they did to this place! I remember when Daddy would bring me here, I was maybe eight. He would let me set up my own office in the corner and I would pretend to fill out invoices and answer the phone.*

Why do I say write a screenplay to learn better how to show versus tell?

In screenwriting, you can only give the actors *hints* to how they feel, how they should act, through their **actions** and their **words**, as in the above bit of dialog. You need to make this clear, because once you turn the script over to the production company, you are essentially leaving the interpretation to the actors and the directions to the director. The clearer the hints, and the more tightly tied to the story, the less the chances of the actors taking your tragedy and turning it into a comedy, or turning your anti-war protest piece into a "nuke 'em all and let God sort 'em out" sort of aggressive statement.

If Lisa walked in, looked around, shrugged, and said, "Good riddance," would you think she is upset at the desecration of her last memories of her father? Uh .... no!

Printed versions of screenplays can be found in libraries. Or professionally published versions of famous screenplays can be found at bookstores, or as part of memorabilia. I used to have a script for **Return of the Jedi** just full of production art and still shots from the movie. Or go online and type "Screenplays" into your search engine, and you'll find a good assortment of places to get free copies of screenplays of your favorite movies. Download them, read them, and study them to see how it's done. Then apply those principles when you write a scene for a book. Later, you can go back and insert things like memories, feelings, thoughts, to flesh out what your characters are **showing** through their actions and words.

Do Yourself a Favor: Tips and Quips on the Writing Life

FILLING IN THE WHITE SPACES

Have you ever thought about all that white space on a standard screenplay page?

Why do they waste so much paper, indenting the dialog on both sides, inserting parentheticals that are indented even more, in the dialog?

Part of that is to help with estimating timing, to know how long the screenplay is going to be. Standard formatted screenplays translate to about one minute of screen time per page of script. Of course, you have to allow for some variation, depending on how much action there is versus how much dialog. A long exchange of snappy one-liners between two or three characters, with not much else happening on camera, might take less than one minute per page. In an action-intensive movie, a single line, such as "Bandit's car races up the incline, dodging a long line of state trooper cars and jumps the river, hitting Buford's Cadillac with his back wheels as he lands," could take up two, three, four minutes on the screen -- depending on whether the director decided that scene needed to be done in slow motion to get all the impact he wanted.

So what is all that white space for, anyway? That's what the director and actors fill in when they take the movie from script to screen, all the choices and designs for sets and costumes and characters and special effects and action. That's what **you** have to fill in, when you're translating your screenplay into a novel. When I turned my screenplay originally titled, *The Wolf Trail*, into **Charli**, a Quarry Hall book, the screenplay took up 100 pages on my computer. It almost tripled in word count, yet the page count increased only by half, by the time I was done.

I filled in the white space -- getting inside the characters' heads and senses, showing how they felt, what they were thinking, what sensory impressions they experienced, and giving readers back story and memories. A line of script says, "Bright summer morning," as it sets the stage, but in the book, I can go on for a paragraph or two, describing the chill in the air, the dampness lingering from the storm the night before, the smell of mud, the colors of the leaves and flower petals scattered across the lawn, the scent of coffee brewing in the next room, the rumpled bed from the heroine's restless night, the books scattered across the office floor, where a gust of wind knocked a window open and pushed the books off the shelf. On and on. Why describe the scene? To put the characters **there** in the middle of it, so they feel like they're there, with all their senses.

On a film set, the artistic director and the people in charge of props and costumes and stunts and makeup and effects create everything for the audience to see. You, as writer, get to do all those jobs with just words. You could just say, "Jasmine walked into the room," but your character would in essence be acting in a blank room. Would you sit through a movie where characters walked through empty rooms, no color, no sounds, no furniture, no props? Or worse, a movie where things and people suddenly appeared a second before they were needed or someone had to join a conversation? Unless this is some sort of experimental, existential manifesto about the transitory state of life ... hmm, ain't gonna work. I think I'd get a headache watching all that popping in (and maybe out again, when they're no longer needed) on screen. I'd be confused, at the very least, besides it smacking of *deus ex machina*. (No, if you still don't know what that means, I'm not going to explain that. Go look it up. Or ask a theater major if you have one handy.)

I don't know about you, but I **hate** reading scenes where you had no idea there were other people in the room until they entered the conversation, or you had no idea the characters were in the kitchen until someone reached over and poured himself a cup of coffee. You wouldn't watch a movie like that -- so don't make your readers endure a book like that. A saying in theater is that if a gun will go off in Act III, it better be on the stage in Act I. (Conversely, don't tease or mislead readers/the audience by having a gun visible in Act I, but it isn't used by Act III.) The same applies with writing books. If someone is going to join a conversation, if a piece of furniture or some other item is going to be necessary to the discussion or action coming up, readers need to know those people are there *before* they start talking or the props are used. Otherwise you're basically playing in a holodeck, where the computer drops things on you a second before you need them. I don't know about you, but that'd get pretty irritating if the gaming computer kept helping my opponent every time I had him backed into a corner and took the advantage away from me. Know what I mean?

- ✓ *Do Yourself A Favor*: Don't make a practice of constantly changing the rules. Don't stack the deck against your readers. Don't wear them out with all sorts of little surprises, so that by the time you get to big surprises you absolutely need to have show up in the book, they're irritated and unable to feel surprise. Make sense?

Fill In The Blank Spaces: set the stage, fill in the details, let them know what your characters are feeling, seeing, smelling, hearing, tasting, thinking, remembering.

While all those details can be left to the director and the designers in a movie, that's your job now. Don't give your readers a boring movie. And while yes, it's a good thing to engage them so they use their imaginations when reading your book, you're in trouble if your characters suddenly break the image your readers created in their heads because you gave them no clues whatsoever. Say readers imagine your heroine is a tiny, curly-haired blonde with pixie-like features and a voice like a lark. Suddenly she picks up and swings a broadsword weighing 200 pounds, and roars out a war cry that makes the rafters shake. Before the reader recovers from that shock, the hero shouts to his sidekick, "Who is that raven-haired Amazon covered in blue and scarlet tattoos?"

As a side note: Filling in those details helps you in arguments with the cover artist, who tries to save time by slapping pre-existing art on your cover, and insists that's what your main character looks like. If you have enough details already established in the book, you can win the argument. Of course, you'll probably have to pay more for original artwork, or find a new cover artist, but that's a topic for another rant ...

Some surprises are good for readers, but not when your story constantly conflicts with the images they've been painting in their imaginations -- they had to, because you didn't give them any details. This is **your** playground they've been invited into, and **your** imagination movie they're watching. Make sure they see and hear and taste and smell and feel and experience the emotions and memories and thoughts that **you** did, when you wrote the story. **No Blank Spaces, Please!**

Michelle L. Levigne

JALAPENOS = BACKSTORY

What do jalapenos have to do with writing? Specifically, with backstory? (Yeah, I mentioned them before. Time to expand on it.)

First off, do you know what backstory is? Essentially, it's the texture that gives your characters three dimensions, makes them seem real -- gives your readers the feeling your characters existed before they picked up the book, and will continue to live on and have adventures after the story ends and they close the book.

Backstory explains -- ideally, **shows** -- why your character does the things she does, says the things he says, reacts the way she does, makes the choices he makes, because of the things that happened to her, the things he learned, the things she did ... in the past.

Backstory should be *dusted* into your story, not dropped in huge globs and mountains. The technical term is "data dump" or "info dump."

Treat your backstory like jalapeno peppers. Just a little bit, in tiny pieces, scattered evenly through your story, adds just the right seasoning and body and texture.

Too much, in chunks that are too large, and the backstory can overpower the entire story. It can slow down the pace -- because honestly, how quickly can you eat a dish that tastes of nothing but jalapenos?

Most important, if you don't handle backstory carefully -- like jalapenos -- you can give your readers good reason to put down the book, push it away, and never come back. Worse, they might just decide that you're such a heavy-handed "cook," they will be hesitant to try anything else that might come out of your kitchen/imagination.

Do Yourself a Favor: Tips and Quips on the Writing Life

CONSISTENCY IS SURVIVAL

In editing, one of my big pet peeves, maybe the biggest one, is CONSISTENCY.

Character names:

I edited a YA book where, in the first *two* pages, one character was referred to as Mom, Mummy, Mother, Timmy's mother, Mrs. Wilson, Grace Wilson ... see where I'm going? If the reader isn't paying attention, she'll think there are **five** different characters on the page with Timmy. Uh, wouldn't that be confusing to you? I'm not saying that other characters in the story can't refer to that person by different names -- that reflects their relationship with the character. Timmy sure wouldn't call his mother "Mrs. Wilson" or "Grace," but wouldn't he refer to her by one name? He wouldn't switch back and forth between "Mom," "Mummy," and "Mother," would he? You, as narrator, should refer to the character by one name, so readers know all the time who you're referring to.

I edited another book where a character was referred to as Dr. Smithers for the first three-quarters of the book -- then all of a sudden the narrator started talking about Andrew. Who was Andrew? When did he enter the story? It took three pages of wondering before another character referred to Andrew as Dr. Andrew Smithers, when it finally clicked.

✓ *Do Yourself A Favor*: Don't Confuse Your Readers!

Another consistency issue I face regularly deals with mechanics, and especially editing books by Christian authors. In one paragraph, they reference a Bible verse as "2 Corinthians 6:12." A paragraph later, they write the reference as "II Peter 1:5." Then a paragraph later, the reference is "the book of Daniel, second chapter, verse twelve." Or the author puts the Bible verse in italics and indents from both sides with the reference after the verse one-third of the time, and the rest of the time leaves off the italics or the indents or both, and sometimes puts the reference before the verse.

See the inconsistencies? Decide on the format you're going to use for referencing things like Bible verses, or books and authors you're quoting from, and **stick with it**. Say you quote from an author, and directly after the quote you insert a footnote with the bibliography information in it. Fine. The next time you quote someone, don't put that bibliography info in parentheses. **Be Consistent**. Either all footnotes, or all parentheses.

Another issue is capitalizing (or not) pronouns for God, or when addressing the members of the Trinity: He, Him, His, Them, They, Their, You, Your. I prefer to capitalize, as a measure of respect. However, this is something the author needs to decide if he is self-publishing. If he is being published by a publisher, large or small or micro, he must follow the house style. Too many times when I'm editing someone, they start out lowercasing the pronouns for God, then one chapter is capitalized, then they go back to lowercase. Usually when that happens, I either stick with the formatting the book started out with, or I determine what is in the majority. But what do I do when the author starts out with both capitalization and lowercasing in the same paragraph -- or even the same sentence? Usually when that happens, I tell the author: *Be consistent. I can't decide what the majority is, so you have to decide and make the corrections.* I can just imagine they don't like that. Umm, sorry, but I'm not going to make the decision, because with my luck, it will always be the opposite of what the author decides he wants to do!

(When you do make the corrections, please, do not take the lazy way out and do a universal search-and-replace. For example, if you change every "he" to "He," guess what happens? Every single word with "he" in it, either at the start or the middle, will suddenly have "He" in it. Even the instances when the "he" you're referring to isn't God! Which turns into a bigger mess that will take longer to fix -- especially if you again do the universal search-and-replace. When you do the search-and-replace, do it one word at a time. It will be tedious, but you will save yourself a lot of misery or embarrassment in the long run. Just sayin' ...)

When you're being published by a traditional publisher, there are standards you have to follow. Some publishers don't like sentences that start with conjunctions, or a publisher will insist that all pronouns referencing God be capitalized, and another refuses to allow that, and another publisher wants 1 and 2 in front of Peter, Corinthians, Thessalonians, etc., while another insists on I and II. That's the choice of the publisher, meaning you have to follow the rules. If you don't make the required changes, the publisher will either do it for you or keep sending the book back until you fall into line and abide by the terms of the contract you signed, which does give them authority and final say over your book (and probably not give you another book contract, if you're considered a problem author). If you don't want to follow the rules, or you get ticked when they make the changes you refused to make, save yourself a lot of aggravation and just get another publisher. (Don't want another publisher? Then pull up your big-boy pants and follow the rules. And work hard to get really popular and a best-seller, so you can dictate changes in the contract.)

However, in self-publishing, **You** are the publisher. You establish the standards. Once the mechanics are taken care of, it's all up to you. Just please be **consistent**.

Do Yourself a Favor: Tips and Quips on the Writing Life

USE YOUR OWN VOCAB, PLEASE?

Every once in a while, I get an editing job where it is oh, so painfully clear that the writer is trying to use a vocabulary that he or she does not possess or use on a regular basis. They're someone with a lemonade vocabulary, but trying to talk with champagne words. You know what I mean?

Instead of using words they know, words they use every day, they reach for the fancy, multi-syllabic ones that they think will get people to pay attention and take their books seriously. What's worse, they don't know how to fully and properly use a thesaurus. They go to the thesaurus, and instead of using the words at the top of the list, the ones most often used, the ones people will understand without having to reach for their own thesaurus ... these wannabe literary geniuses pick the most obscure word tied to that meaning. What's worse, they use a noun when they need an adjective, because they don't know how to use that specific word. Or they try to turn an adverb into a verb. Even if the readers don't understand the word, instinctively, something clanks.

Be honest with yourself: How many times are you going to be willing to reach for your dictionary or go to the search engine on your phone to look up a word before you decide the author is a pretentious twit? Your next action is to close the book, never to open it again. You send it back to the library or put it in the box to go to the used bookstore to be traded in, or delete the file from your e-reader.

Why would you want to do that to other readers -- and worse, condemn your beloved brain-child (your book), the result of thousands of hours of thought and effort and sweat and tears, to the same treatment?

These people searching for fancy, literati-impressing vocabularies do not make themselves look highly educated and la-de-da. What they do instead is make themselves look ridiculous. Do you know who Mrs. Malaprop is? She's a character in an old English drama who used words that sounded "almost" right for what she meant. For instance, someone says "perspective" when they actually mean "prospective." Or in a recent book I edited, the phrase was, "His actions were admiral." I was pretty sure the author meant "admirable." Or a book I read recently, where people kept "clamoring" over hills and "clamored" into the saddle -- sorry, but clamor = noise or making an appeal, while **clamber** = climb. **sigh** You know what the writers mean, because the words sound a lot like the right ones -- but you also know they're using the *wrong* word.

That's where the comedy/frustration comes in. (I really do have to start a file of these silly gaffs, to bring up for future examples.) Frustration: if those glaring grammatical and wrong-word-choice errors continue, people pick them up and use them, and spread them, and they become commonplace. To harken back to previous rants: "try and" is **wrong**!!! Yet "everybody" seems to be saying and writing "try and" when the proper word combination is "try to," so the error continues, reinforced by constant -- incorrect --- usage.

> ✓ *Do Yourself A Favor*: Don't contribute to the continuing, increasing speed of the dumbing down of American English.

Do you want your book to be considered a joke? Humorous? Amusing? If it's not on purpose, then don't do a Malaprop.

Or worse, readers who notice these errors decide you really don't care about your writing. It's a sloppy mess that you dumped into the computer and then before the pixils on the screen cooled down, you shot the file off to a website, a blog, a publisher who didn't care toad squat about proper grammar, spelling, punctuation, or context, and it was published. Or, what probably happens more often than editors and publishers want to admit, the author is a prima donna who believes his/her writing is pure gold and has a hissy if the editor changes one word. Even if the author misspelled his/her *own name* ... (yep, seen it happen!)

The language in your book should sound as close to the way you actually talk as possible -- but with the grammar corrected, of course. Trying to sound like a dry-as-dust academic, or use enough purple prose and sugary imagery to put someone into diabetic shock when you're actually someone who likes shoot-em-up adventure with a large dash of humor thrown in?

Just.
Don't.

On the other hand, if you know your vocabulary needs expanding, then do it naturally -- read the type of books you want your writing to emulate. Change the way you talk. Do it gradually. If you want to change your vocabulary from nickel and dime words to fifty-cent pieces, **earn** the vocabulary. Get used to using those words. Hang around with people who use those words, so you see them "in action" and can make them part of you by osmosis. Don't wear a mask.

Readers will know you're not being honest, and it will make your story come off as plastic, posed, contrived (insert here your favorite synonym for fake/blech).

Do Yourself a Favor: Tips and Quips on the Writing Life

DO YOU HOP?

Some time ago, I had to do major writing surgery, turning a fan novel I wrote decades ago into the pilot/launch novel for a hopeful new SF series. I hadn't read this story in years, and had to reacquaint myself with what I wrote. Besides changing all the character and technology and place names, the first go-through was just to make note in my mind of all the story holes, and the major changes in the society I would have to make (as in no alien races, everybody is Human, so some major plot points and "revelations" had to be dropped and/or changed).

I was in pain before I was halfway through the revision. Not because of typos, small holes in sub-plots, not following up on implied promises, forgetting to tell readers who was talking, or other stupid glitches. (Hey, I wrote this more than thirty years ago!)

No, I was in agony because I caught **myself** head-hopping.

I started a scene in one person's POV (that's point of view, for those who don't know writer lingo) and then included a paragraph or two in someone else's POV, and then shifted to a third POV. For instance (this was a Star Trek fan novel, once upon a time), a Klingon came into his commander's office with some news. I took a sentence to tell readers how much he despised his superior and couldn't wait to trick him into a major mistake so he would be removed from authority -- and knowing the Klingons, probably from life, too.

Then in the next paragraph, I revealed the commander knew what his underling thought of him and he wasn't worried because he had a lot of powerful people on his side, and he despised the young upstart and was looking for a way to embarrass his powerful sponsors in the military.

In my defense, I wrote this when I had very little training and very few books on writing, no teachers up to that point other than **Writer's Digest.** *And just because I did it, and really didn't get caught, except by myself later on, does not make it all right for everybody else to head-hop.*

Like I ask people I edit, **how** does your POV character know what someone else is thinking or feeling? Is your POV character telepathic? Unless this is a science fiction or fantasy novel and invading other people's thoughts is a major plot element, **don't** head-hop. Stay in the POV of the person who starts the scene. That means you cannot ever tell us what another character is thinking or feeling or planning to do, because the POV character doesn't have any way of knowing **unless** you head-hop (or your POV character is not only telepathic, but ignores all the rules of ethics for psionic gifts and the use thereof).

Unless you're a big-time, bestselling author who can handle head-hopping without confusing readers, do not try this trick at home. All my publishers insist on staying to one POV per scene. If you absolutely must shift POV because it is essential to tell readers what another character is thinking, or the POV character leaves the scene but the scene continues, then either break the scene (starting a new chapter is a great way/place to do it) or make it very, very, very clear you're shifting to a new person's POV. Then **stay** in that POV until the end of the scene.

Unless you have long ears and a puffy tail, NO hopping!

Do Yourself a Favor: Tips and Quips on the Writing Life

HOW DID HE KNOW THAT?
(Head-hopping rant redux)

Allow me to continue to grip about something frustrating I see in books by beginners as well as people who should know better: Telepathy.

"Huh?" you may ask. (Especially if you read and write SF or fantasy books, like I do, where such talents are considered not only possible, but vital to the story's progression.)

- ✓ *Do Yourself A Favor*: Be very clear from the moment you first put pen to paper, or fingers to keyboard, if this is a book with psionic gifts of any kind, including telepathy. If this is not a fantasy or SF novel: **No Mind Reading Allowed**!

(Well, okay, if this is spiritual warfare, where such gifts are usually brought on by demon possession or angelic interference, then that might be allowed. But honestly, wouldn't you class those books under fantasy?)

A very simple, crude illustration of what I mean by telepathy is a scene where the POV character is Tom. We see the scene through his eyes. We know what he's thinking. We know what comes through his physical senses. Usually (not always -- there are always exceptions) fiction is told in past tense, through the eyes of one narrator or POV character at a time. Yes, there are some writers who tell you what's going on in everyone's head at the same time, but I find such writers really, really confusing. They seem to think they're God.

Tom occupied his time in the waiting room watching Gregory, who got hungrier the longer he waited and made things worse by thinking about nearby restaurants and their menus.

Excuse me, *how* does Tom know Gregory is hungry and is thinking about nearby restaurants? Without being able to read Gregory's mind? Has Gregory spoken aloud, has his stomach grumbled, has he started flipping through the phone book and saying the names of restaurants aloud? How does Tom know what Gregory is thinking if he's not a telepath or a wizard?

Another illustration:

Sharon was busy with the Monday baking, happily remembering her childhood learning to bake from her grandmother, when George walked in. He didn't see her there, distracted by fuming about the fight he had last week with Rick. He kicked the cabinet, making the flour canister fall down on his foot and breaking two toe bones.

How does Sharon know George is fuming about Rick, and two bones are broken? "Fuming" implies inner dialog, not spoken, so she can't hear him muttering his thoughts, for instance. For that matter, even if we accept that George has become the POV character (not just head-hopping, but doing it in the same paragraph), how does he know he has two broken bones? Is he a doctor, so he knows just from the shrieking of pain in his foot that he has broken bones instead of just bruised and bleeding flesh?

Always keep the impressions, the thoughts, the emotions in the perspective of the person who is showing the reader the scene. Unless you're reading science fiction or fantasy or horror, where people have the ability to either broadcast whatever they're thinking and feeling, or invade the thoughts of other people so they know what is going through their minds, always ask yourself, and your POV character: How does he **know** that about the other character?

You know what I consider even worse than head-hopping that implies telepathy?

TIME TRAVEL

No, not the H.G. Wells version of time travel, or what they did in Star Trek or Stargate: SG-1. I'm talking about head-hopping that turns into time travel, because that's the only way to explain how the head-hopping could occur.

It starts with the POV character sitting down and thinking, remembering something momentous that happened in his life, many years ago.

Ferdinand leaned back in his wheelchair and gazed out across the snow-covered gardens that stretched to the horizon. He remembered when he would have been out there, enjoying all that knee-deep, white splendor. When he was a child, barely tall enough to see over those drifts that threatened to bury the fountain, he would have been out there building snowman after snowman, blissfully happy with the task, blissfully uncaring that each one looked just like the other.

A few years later, when he was taller, he would have been on the slopes just beyond that barrier of tall rhododendrons, maybe fumbling through learning to use the skis Mother got him for his twelfth birthday. Callie, the gardener's daughter, was four years older than him, and had been glad to teach him what she knew. At sixteen she was heading for the Olympics, and she found some enjoyment in watching the owner's son learning the sport she loved. Ferdy was a good kid, still not spoiled rotten by his step-father's attempts to buy his loyalty, and she hoped he would stay like his mother and not let that arrogant jerk make him over in his image. Callie still ached at the loss of Mr. Sullivan. He had treated all the staff like family, and had insisted on paying for her skiing lessons when she first showed her talent.

See what happened? Halfway through the paragraph, the viewpoint shifted from Ferdinand's to Callie's. That's bad enough when the story is in the present, but this scene is in Ferdinand's *memories* -- yet shifted to Callie's viewpoint. That's time travel, and pretty tricky time travel, too.

- ✓ *Do Yourself A Favor*: STAY looking through ONE set of eyes in each scene.

If it's vital to show readers Callie's memories of a scene that Ferdinand remembered, then you need to make it believable for her to be remembering the same scene. For instance, once Ferdinand finishes remembering, he could get on the phone and call Callie. Let's say she's at the lodge she bought with her winnings from years of competition, and now she's training her grandchildren for the Olympics. The scene cuts and shifts to Callie picking up the phone. As soon as Ferdinand tells her what he had been thinking about, her memory video can begin playing.

Make sense?

Michelle L. Levigne

ARE YOU AN OBJECT OR A SUBJECT?
(Previous rant revisited and expanded)

Does it bother you when people use objects when they should use subjects?

And if it doesn't, **Why Not?**

Too many times, in too many places, in the mouths or pens of people who should know better, I hear something like this: "They interviewed Joe and I." "The list of guests included Grace and I." "The class gave going away gifts to the Petersons and I."

Umm ... NO!

People who say things like this are confusing **objects** and **subjects**. Maybe they think they're sounding "proper" and educated, as if "I" is refined while "me" is vulgar ... but ... it's still wrong!

When you are the one acting, then you can say "I" -- you're the **subject**. But when something is **done to you**, you are the **object** and you say "me."

How do you know when to use "I" and when to use "me"?

Easy test: Take the other person out of the sentence!

Would you say, "They interviewed I"? No, you'd say, "They interviewed *me*." "The list of guests included *me*." "The class gave *me* a going away present." Etc.

When you get it right with the object and subject with just one person in the sentence, then you can insert other people. ***What's right when you are alone in the sentence does not change when more people show up.***

Writers are the guardians of language, of clear communication. If we don't get things like this right, how can we expect everybody else to take us seriously when we tell them about other broken grammar rules that drive us nuts?

Get the little things right, otherwise you have no right to holler about the big, stupid, glaring mistakes.

Do Yourself a Favor: Tips and Quips on the Writing Life

"BLEAH," "MEH," OR "YEAH!" ?

I edited an academic research paper that the author decided he would publish in book form to elucidate and educate and inform and enlighten others who are interested in and curious about and longing to explore the same question and conundrum and mystery that he explored.

Got lost in all that convoluted language? Yeah, and I was afraid his readers would be lost in his academic, dry, repetitive, formulaic reporting. There is a vast difference between writing to conform to the style and patterns of academia (and please your doctoral committee), and writing for ordinary readers. I had to ask the author: Who is your audience for this book? More academics? Or ordinary readers from many walks of life who just want to know what you found out? More than half the book was spent on discussing the research methods he used, the philosophies behind the development of those methods, and how he went about obtaining his sources. If his audience was strictly academics who care about the **how** just as much as (or even more than) the **what**, then he would be fine. But if he was aiming at an audience who just wanted to know **what** he learned, and didn't care **how**, then he was in trouble.

So to repeat myself (but from a different angle): **Know Your Audience**. Who are you writing for? What do they want to read? What are their tastes? What are they expecting when they open up your book?

That means knowing the proper labels to put on your book. Sure, romances sell big, but you can't write vampire-hunters-in-the-Old-West-meet-time-travelers-who-fall-through-to-the-time-of-dinosaurs, label it as a romance (when there is nary a longing look or kiss), and then expect readers to just devour it. The ones who like romances are going to be disgusted, and the ones who want vampires, time travel, and dinosaurs won't be looking for it in the romance aisle. (Unless, of course, they're willing to put up with romance overshadowing the vampires, time travel, and dinosaurs.)

What reaction are you going for?

Bleah = you didn't give me what I wanted, you didn't follow through on your promise, I'm going to avoid your writing from now on.

Meh = okay, you kinda gave me what you promised, but it wasn't what I was looking for, not what I enjoy, I *might* give you another chance (If I get the book at a discount next time), but don't disappoint me again.

Yeah! = you followed through on your promises, it was what I was looking for, it was a lot of fun, I am definitely putting you on my "must read more" list. AND I'm gonna tell my friends. (That last part is really important -- and you don't want to get the "I'm gonna tell my friends" reaction when they despise your book, and maybe you, too.)

An apocryphal story from a writing conference has an editor for a major romance publisher telling about a query letter she got. Essentially the author said, "Romance is garbage, nobody wants to read it, I have a book full of blood and destruction and a tough guy who doesn't have time for stupid women. Buy my book and you'll make a million." That author didn't know the publisher, didn't know the market, and definitely didn't know how to write a query that would make the editor say, "Yeah!"

On a side note, and not an apocryphal story: I was at a weeklong writing boot camp for SF and fantasy writers. One of the assistant staffers, who had frequently indicated she thought she was "all that," announced she had heard there was a lot of money in "that romance stuff." So she was going to sit down and "toss out a couple bodice-rippers." Those words clearly showed she had no respect for or knowledge of the genre. The label of "bodice-ripper" is a joke and a derogatory term. People *outside* romance use the label, not insiders. She got snotty when I pointed out that I wrote romance, and people in the industry didn't use the term "bodice-ripper." She knew better, of course. Her attitude showed she had even less respect for her intended audience than she did for the genre itself.

Don't make her mistake. Readers are savvy. Readers are sensitive. Readers can tell when a writer is writing for profit alone, or if they're writing because they love the genre. While a book might be technically perfect, if the spirit or heart of a book is off-key or missing altogether, you're going to get a "meh" or a "bleah" or even a "You wasted my time and money, your name is mud!" reaction.

So what am I saying? You may be a great story teller, but it won't do you any good if you don't respect the genre, if the book isn't labeled properly or it isn't brought to the attention of people who want to read that particular type of story. Know your market, know your readers. Give them what they want. Make them say, "**Yeah!**"

FAIR USE -- EMPHASIS ON *FAIR*

In a handful of books I've edited, the authors have quoted songs and poems. Almost without exception, they quote the **entire** song or poem. Almost without exception, they don't mention the name of the author or composer or publisher or copyright date. Sometimes not even the title.

Now, that's just plain rude!

(Don't get me started on the people who quote a song inaccurately, changing words, or even merging two different songs together. There's this thing called the Internet, where you can do a search for the correct lyrics/author's/composer's name/title /copyright date/whether it's in public domain or not. NO excuse for not knowing.)

How would you feel if something you wrote was quoted in someone else's book or article and you didn't get credit?

More important than that, it's a violation of copyright law. Consider this: You read a book, you come across a poem, and if credit isn't given to another author, don't you assume the author of the book wrote the poem? So in effect, quoting someone's song or poem without giving them credit is plagiarism (a fancy word for stealing -- and lying). It's about as tacky as buying a pre-made Thanksgiving dinner and then telling your guests you did all the cooking yourself.

"But what about Fair Use?" you may ask.

Fair Use allows you to use a **small** portion of a work without the permission of the author or other copyright holders -- <u>but you still have to give credit</u>. Defining what that small portion is ... that's way up in the air. No one can agree, because it really isn't spelled out. *Thanks for the help, lawmakers...*

What percentage of the whole are you using? Four paragraphs from a 100,000-word book is a fraction of a percent, while one line from a poem is a huge chunk. It's all proportions and percentages. Would you put the entire manuscript of **War and Peace** into your book? Then don't use the entire poem or song you want to quote.

Not without permission, anyway.

If the material you want to quote is in public domain, <u>say so</u>, and feel free to quote the whole thing. If it is **not** in public domain, then you must, on pain of death or financial devastation or public humiliation get permission. I'm sure some of the people I edited sighed and rolled their eyes and decided to ignore me when I gave them that advice, and told them about copyright law and Fair Use Doctrine. Or they had a hissy when they "wasted" time finding out the name of the author and publisher. Even worse for them, they went through the process to ask permission and were told they had to pay a fee.

My advice: Paraphrase the message of the song or poem if it is important to your story. Give the title and author/composer in natural conversation in your story, if you can, or at least relate that information in the character's thoughts, so readers look it up. Don't take the chance that the author won't learn you used her poem or song without permission. Because guess what? Authors and publishers can and do sue for copyright infringement. Even if they're nice, understanding people, and they know you didn't intend to do them any harm, they *have to* take legal action to protect themselves in the future. If they let your copyright violation slide, they could lose the right to sue the next intellectual property thief who does them real damage. At the very least, their complaint will lose its power because they let *you* get away with it. They need to protect their intellectual property, and protect their ability to do so.

Side note: This is general practice, advice I picked up while proofreading for a legal publishing company, reading all sorts of essays on intellectual property law and trademarks and copyright and related topics. Do not take it as legal advice or rock-solid guidelines. Always ask a professional, someone who deals with copyright law and intellectual property matters on a regular basis. Not every lawyer or journalism professor will have the info you need to keep you out of trouble. You wouldn't go to a lawnmower service to fix your Ferrari, would you?

If quoting the material word-for-word is vital for the story or article, then bite the bullet and pay the fee. I can guarantee it's a lot cheaper than paying a lawyer, on top of the penalties demanded by the publisher and the injured author. Plus there's the long-term damage to your reputation and career that you suffer when word gets around that you're a plagiarist. No publisher wants to to risk their reputation and finances on a proven thief.

Still think that asking permission is a great big pain and inconvenience? Consider this: what are you going to do if or when people come along and steal *your* stories and poems? You can't turn around and sue them, can you, when you tried to get away with it yourself? Fair is fair.

Bottom line: Using someone else's written work without giving them credit or asking permission is stealing -- and a violation of the Fair Use Doctrine, which is supposed to make things **fair**.

- ✓ *Do Yourself A Favor*: treat other writers and artists in general the way you would want them to treat you.

It's always better to ask, because forgiveness isn't guaranteed. I had a co-worker who always declared, with a big, smug grin: *It's easier to ask forgiveness than ask permission.* Maybe. Until someone decides not to forgive, because you've developed a reputation of always asking forgiveness, and never permission. Just how many times can you get forgiveness before people decide you're not sorry, because you certainly aren't trying to mend your ways?

Another thing: Don't depend on your memory. Look it up. I have caught too many misquotes of fairly well-known quotations. Or the wrong person gets credit. For instance, the author will state, "In the words of John Locke," when the person they are quoting is actually John Donne. Or as stated earlier, people insisting that Pocahontas married John Smith. Or what's worse, misquoting Bible verses, and rewriting Bible history. Self-proclaimed Bible teachers I edited have insisted that David was in the lion's den (not Daniel). Judas was sold into slavery in Egypt (not Joseph). Samuel's mother was Ruth (not Hannah). That's what happens when you don't check your facts, and just rely on your memory.

And for heaven's sake, don't shrug it off by stating in your book, "I don't know where this comes from," because unless you're working somewhere without an Internet connection or access to a public library, you **can** look it up. Or at least ask someone to find the information for you. Stating you can't find the information is flat-out laziness. Readers will know you didn't do your homework because you couldn't be bothered. Irritate readers often enough with such instances of "I won't" badly disguised as "I can't," they'll stop listening to you. The subliminal message is that you can't be trusted.

Funny thing is, people seem to want to be able to trust writers of fiction even more than they want to be able to trust the people who write non-fiction books. Maybe because there's so much un-truth and blatant attempts to rewrite reality nowadays everywhere else.

Truth has to take refuge somewhere -- make sure it's safe in your books.

Michelle L. Levigne
BUTTON HOLES, NOT THE WHOLE DRESS

I once edited a book that should never have been sent to me. It was very evident (to me, anyway) that the author never bothered reading her book after she dumped her rambling thoughts into the computer -- and probably quit school after flunking second grade a dozen times. The grammar, spelling and punctuation mistakes were headache-inducing.

Bottom line: She had no right sending it to the publisher, expecting someone to fix the mangled drivel. In the age of texting and instant messaging and email, this alleged author could barely grasp the essentials of conversation. Forget the ego-trip of expecting people to read 50,000 words of reporting in excruciating detail every conversation and text message as her life and career and shallow relationships fell apart. Yeah, I could see why her life fell apart -- she put as little effort into the people around her as she put into her communication skills. Even worse, she was over forty years old, and talked like a middle schooler, punctuating every paragraph, and sometimes every other sentence with, "I was like, wow!" "I was like, cosmic!" "I was like, amazing!"

What does "I was like" actually *mean*?

I believe the writing talent is a stewardship. And that means no matter how brilliant you *imagine* your book is, you still have a responsibility to go through it and make it the best it can be before you "release it into the world." That means even **before** you send it to an editor to "fix" it for you.

Several years ago on the EPIC loop, one of the authors griped about having to "waste" his time and energy (better spent doing what, exactly?) to fix punctuation, grammar, spelling, and formatting. "Isn't that what editors are for? To fix all those things for me? Why should I waste my time?" Needless to say, he got pounded by the editors and publishers on the loop.

Consider the heavy load of submissions that editors in all levels of publishing receive. If your story is equal to someone else's in terms of the suspense and characterization and details, and there is only room for **one** book in the next available publishing slot, the editor will consider how much time she will have to invest in polishing one manuscript versus the other. Guess who she'll buy? If you guessed "the book that requires the least amount of work from her," you're right.

Your editor (whether the in-house editor, or someone like me who polishes up vanity press manuscripts, or helps an author polish and revise before submitting to that overworked, finicky editor) is **not** there to, in essence, write your book for you. I'm the tailor who puts on the buttons and trims the button holes and fixes the hems. I am **not** there to take whole panels out of your dress, find new material to change the look, change a neck to a sleeve, on and on. You should have your book as close to the finished product as possible before you send it to me. I'm there to clean things up, not change baby doll pajamas into an evening gown!

If you want an editor who does that kind of work, baby, it'll **cost** you. You might have to put someone else's name on your book with yours. After all, that editor did as much work as you did. Maybe more. Bottom line: ideas are a dime a dozen, but the talent to actually write a book that people will read -- all the way to the end, without throwing it against the wall -- that is a priceless and (sadly) rare talent.

Don't write a book -- don't make a dress -- until you understand what all the tools do and why they are necessary, what each type of material works best, and where it works best. And for heaven's sake, don't go out in public without making sure your dress doesn't have huge, gaping holes in it!

Michelle L. Levigne

GET TO THE END!

> You can't have a booksigning without a published book. (Makes sense, right?)
> You can't have a published book until you've checked the galleys.
> You don't get galleys until you've gone through the torturous editing process with your editor.
> Can't have the editing done until you turn in the book designated by a contract.
> Can't get that contract until you send the book to the editor -- and you can't send it until you query and gain the editor's interest.
> You can't query a book until you have one to send in!

Of course, once you're a published author, you can work up to the point, either with a really good sales record, or just a good relationship with the editor, where you can simply say, "I have this idea ..." and essentially sell the book before you write it. But that takes time.

What am I getting at? Bear with me...

You need to have a finished book to query it (until you're so successful that people are clamoring [not clambering] to buy scribbled notes on a wet napkin).

So **FINISH** the dang book!

To finish the book you have to do multiple revisions and polishes.

You can't revise and polish a book until you ... that's right, say it along with me ... **finish** that first draft.

I have a friend who I consider a much better writer. She has hundreds of scenes scribbled out for dozens of possible books. Lovely bits of dialog and action, and plot movement ... but those dozens of scenes haven't been sewn together into a cohesive whole.

You probably have writing friends who do the same thing. Or maybe you're the one with the problem. "But I want the scene to be *perfect* before I go on to the next one." Excuse me, but that's what **revisions** are for. Sometimes I only have a general idea where the book is going. I have a beginning and an end in sight, but the journey from A to B is kind of misty. The wandering and working your way out of the mist is the *fun* part of the process. Getting to know your characters, their pasts and foibles and fears. Going off on tangents. Discovering things you didn't know or didn't even imagine about your characters when you first sat down to write the book.

You can't go on that journey until you get moving. So what if the scene you just finished writing doesn't feel right, there are missing pieces, and maybe you're not sure where it belongs in the story? Keep moving. Give yourself permission to do a half-baked scene and go on to the next one. You might just find out what you need to fix scene 27 when you get to scene 35. Something happens in scene 41, and you realize you need to go back and drop hints and insert props and create a new character in scenes 4, 15, and 23. (No, I don't number my scenes, I'm just saying this to make a point. So don't start numbering your scenes just because you think I do it -- unless that technique works for you.)

So make some notes of what to do and **keep writing**. Get to the end of the book. When you have a better idea of what's going to happen, and what you need to have happen, and what needs to be foreshadowed and what needs to be cut, then you go back and *revise*. The first draft is the skeleton, not the final product.

- ✓ *Do Yourself A Favor:* Give yourself permission to write a first draft (not **part** of a first draft, but the whole thing) that is so utterly wretched, if you printed it out and lined a bird cage, the bird would die. (Kudos to Anne Lamott, who started the original image.)

You can only get better from there. And isn't that a good feeling?

- ✓ *Do Yourself a Favor:* **Finish The Draft You're Working On.** Doesn't have to be perfect, just has to be there so you have *something* to revise and add to. You can fix a bad scene, but you can't fix a blank page ... except by writing on it.

Michelle L. Levigne
NEVER THROW OUT ANYTHING
Re-use, Recycle.

Okay, I'm going to start out with a confession: Contrary to what I'm going to tell you, I **have** thrown out some of my first stories.

Why? Because they're so raw, so stupid, so badly plotted, so embarrassing, I do not want this dreck hanging around to be found after I'm dead.

Putting that consideration aside ... **don't** (as a general rule) throw out anything you've written.

(Just make sure that it's put somewhere with some plastic explosive and a deadman switch, so it self-destructs the minute your heart stops. If you're worried about people knowing just how awful your first dozen short stories or poems or songs or scripts were. Just saying ...)

Why keep this embarrassing stuff around?

You can **re-use** it someday.

Because right now, I'm kicking myself over a Star Trek novel that I started writing -- longhand, on legal pads, back before I had a computer. I say "started" because I never got past the third or fourth legal pad. I eventually threw it out one day when I decided I didn't want to pursue trying to write for the Star Trek universe. I thought there was nowhere else I could get it published.

Wrong-O!

Now, of course, I have a couple ways I could change the characters and keep the situation, and turn it into something ... interesting. And very clearly not a Trek rip-off.

Everything you've written, no matter how short, no matter if it's an outline, a bungled synopsis, a single scene, a character sketch, a conversation between two unidentified people, or in my case fan fiction of all types ... you can revise it, and use it somewhere else. Recycled. Upgraded and updated. After you've learned enough, gained enough skill, to know why exactly the first version was so awful.

For example ... I wrote a *Highlander* novel (the whole bungled attempt at selling it is proof that a bad, awful, moronic agent is worse than having no agent at all) and later I revised it to turn it into a novel in my Quarry Hall series, **Darcy**. (If you've read **Darcy**, Vincent is basically Duncan, and Joan took a lot of Joe Dawson's lines, and some of Amanda's) A *Stingray* (Stephen Cannell TV show, Nick Mancuso driving a vintage Corvette) fanzine story was expanded and turned into another Quarry Hall book, **Anne's Ogre**. A script for *Highlander* (didn't sell, the know-nothing ex-agent actually had the gall, three months *after* I sent her a TV script, to ask me which studio the script should go to!) was first turned into a fanzine story, and then became the sub-plot and the skeleton for a couple characters for a book in my Commonwealth Universe, **Undying**. A fanzine story I wrote for a friend doing a multi-verse, original fiction 'zine became the germinal seed for the Hoveni (shapeshifter) stories in the Commonwealth Universe. An idea for a script for the USA Network show *Matrix* (no relation to the movies) (Nick Mancuso, driving a modern Corvette) was turned into a fanzine story, and became the basis for the Tabor Heights novel ***The Teddy Bear Dancer***. I wrote a script for the original *MacGyver* series, just before the final half-season. It didn't sell, but I turned it into a feature-length screenplay, and then later the Tabor Heights novel **Wheels**. Another screenplay I wrote for a contest became the basis for the Quarry Hall novel, **Charli**. *The Blue Lotus*, a short story I wrote for a former publisher, for an anthology that was never published became the basis/revised history for the Blue Lotus Society, the good guys/descendants of time travelers in my *Guardians of the Time Stream* Steampunk series. And the second novel in the series, ***The Blue Lotus Society***.

The point of all this? If I didn't hold onto those fan novels and screenplays and failed stories, I wouldn't have had the building blocks for books that eventually were published. I wouldn't have had the skeletons of stories that I adapted and re-sculpted to suit new characters and locations and conflicts. *Besides, no writing is ever wasted. No matter how bad it is, it's practice, it's growth and development of your skill. Look at it this way: manure stinks, but after it sits around long enough, you use it for fertilizer, right? It helps something useful grow.*

✓ *Do Yourself A Favor*: **Don't throw out ANYTHING! EVER!**

Except, yes, the really wretched stuff that will embarrass you and have you turning like a lathe in your coffin, when your family goes through your house after the funeral luncheon ...

Michelle L. Levigne

GET YOURSELF SOME FRESH EYES

No, I'm not talking about investing in Visine or taking a nap before you proofread your story.

I'm talking about finding someone to help you with the final polish. Someone to read through it and find all those little glitches and stupid typos you didn't catch.

Here's the thing: After you've gone through your story a half-dozen times, and your editor went over it two or three times, you both get familiar with what's on the page. You have an idea in your head of what you *want* on the page, how you *want* the book to feel, and the level of clarity. After you've been over your book again and again and again, your mind plays tricks on you. You see the sentences and paragraphs as you *want* them to be, not how they really are. Your brain inserts the right words in there, even if your fingers didn't, and you gloss over the mistakes.

Here's what you need to do:

1 -- Find someone who has not read your story yet. Preferably someone you haven't talked to about the story, either, so they don't have expectations.

2 -- That someone needs to have a good, solid grasp of the rules of grammar, spelling, punctuation -- and the English language!
You might think that's obvious, but it's not -- I've edited plenty of people who speak English as their second or third language, and instead of going to someone who is a native speaker and reader and writer of English, they go to one of their immigrant friends who they consider more skilled with English, and ask them to check the book. Well, chances are good this more skilled friend makes the same grammar, spelling, syntax and punctuation mistakes as the author.

3 -- **Do Not Ask Family Or Friends** to read the manuscript. They'll tell you it's wonderful, don't change a thing. Or they'll focus on stupid little things that aren't wrong. (Or like what happened on *Chesapeake Shores*, they'll read the book looking for themselves.) Because they're your family, odds are they have the same level of education as you, meaning they'll make the same grammar and spelling mistakes you make, so they won't see the mistakes you need them to catch.

For instance, I edited a book where the author's relatives insisted **after** the book was published that the statement, "If you *were* a virgin, you *were* allowed to wear white" (which the author wrote, and was grammatically correct) was wrong, and proper grammar was, "If you *was* a virgin, you *was* allowed to wear white." *sigh*

Do Yourself a Favor: Tips and Quips on the Writing Life

Conjugate the verb "to be" with me: I was; you were; he was; she was; they were; we were.

4 -- **Do not wait** until **after** publication to ask for feedback from your smart, grammatically skilled friends. Do it beforehand, while you still have time to make corrections to the manuscript.

4a -- As a corollary, do not accept or ask for feedback <u>after</u> publication, if you did not ask for help <u>before</u> publication. One writer kept friends and family completely out of the loop on her book. Then, they stood around her at the release party and pointed out all the mistakes they thought she made -- in public! Yeah, really supportive. (NOT!) It was no comfort that none of the mistakes were real mistakes. If they had a chance to give their input beforehand, they wouldn't dare open their mouths about perceived mistakes afterward, because the errors would be on them. Hopefully. Some people can never be satisfied. So why are you hanging with them in the first place?

5 -- When the publisher sends you galley proofs of your book, **this is the time to look for errors and correct them**. This is **not** the time to look at **only** the formatting, and make sure the font is "pretty," and the margins are wide enough, and you like the dingbats between sections. This is the time to fix the **text**. (And make sure you sent the correct manuscript file to the production department.)

- ✓ Do Yourself a Favor: **Ask For Help**, and ask those with the proper skill and experience in writing, in publishing, in grammar/spelling/punctuation to give that help. Would you go to a stonemason for help with making lace? Would you ask someone from a tropical island to help you design clothes to stand up to an Arctic winter?

Michelle L. Levigne
REVISIONS: YES, YOU *MUST*

As a freelance editor, I get books from people whose first books were rejected by traditional publishers. People who never asked why their books were rejected, but decided "rules are for other people" because what they have to say outweighs things like making sure the book is readable. People who wouldn't know proper grammar/spelling/punctuation if it knocked them down and rolled them in the mud and stole their wallets.

A discouraging number of times, I have opened up manuscripts and watched as Word marks all the misspelling and questionable grammar and word choices with the little red and green squiggly lines. Now, these books have been submitted as Word documents, so that means these people *used* Word to write their books. How come they couldn't be bothered to go through the manuscript and at least *try* to correct the spelling mistakes displayed on their screens? Why didn't they use the spell check tool?

Why didn't they read the book at least once, looking for the simple mistakes of spelling, grammar, punctuation? Gaping holes where they changed their husband's name three times, and couldn't keep straight what state they were living in, or made statements such as, "As I discussed earlier," referencing incidents that they never discussed. Or in the case of one author recently, somehow she copied the same text into three different places in the book, completely obliterating large sections of the narrative. One revision or simple "Is it all there?" read-through would have caught so much. Even if they don't know anything about writing and publishing, wouldn't common sense tell them that they should look over what they just created to make sure it says what they want to say, that they didn't leave anything out?

Revise, people. Everyone must revise. Everyone who cares about their writing revises. Best-selling authors revise -- so that means you should, too.

I don't care what your publishing goals are -- this is **your** baby. **You** need to make it the best possible book you can before you hand it off to someone else to tweak the things that got past you, find the logic holes big enough for the *Enterprise* to fly through, and suggest fixes for problems you can't fix even after you've puzzled yourself into a headache. This is **your** baby -- would you let someone else dress your baby in clothes you didn't pick out, dye and cut her hair, paint her toenails, and put makeup on her to suite **their** vision of what she should look like?

That's what happens when you toss a first-draft mess to an editor. His or her vision is going to form your book, no matter how light a touch the editor employs, no matter how hard he or she works to preserve your voice. If the general impression of your manuscript is that you don't care, the editor will take over, and even make major decisions you might not agree with.

Do you want that to happen? NOPE. So give your editor as few reasons as possible to change your book -- give the editor very little that needs fixing.

Revise. Multiple times, if necessary. I still revised this book after I had beta readers go through it. I fixed what they questioned, and then went back again and trimmed. I cut more than 3,000 words after I thought I had the final version done. Revising is necessary!

The closer you are to the starting point in your writing career, the more revisions you need. Granted, you may be unsteady on details of grammar, but doggone it, **use** the spell check program. If you can't figure out that the first word in every sentence should be capitalized, and sentences always end with a period, a question mark or an exclamation point, and punctuation in dialog goes inside quote marks, maybe you shouldn't try to write at this stage. You should be reading dozens and dozens of books to learn from those who know what they're doing. You need to go back to school, pay attention and actually **learn** the basics of grammar, spelling and punctuation.

You may have something important to say with your book, but you must (I cannot emphasize this enough, MUST!) learn to express yourself clearly so that people understand you, before anyone will listen. And that means **revising**.

Michelle L. Levigne
EVEN WHEN IT STOPS BEING FUN?

A long time ago, when I was just getting my feet wet in terms of publishing (and getting lots of rejection letters), I made myself a promise:

"I'll stop writing when it stops being fun."

I had heard enough stories and warnings and read enough industry articles and books on writing, I knew my chances of getting published at all were kind of thin, and then the odds of making decent money were even thinner, and being able to make a living off my writing ... well, the odds were so thin, I could see through them.

So why keep tormenting myself? Why should **you** keep slogging through, sacrificing a social life and family time and money and enduring headaches and frustration for the sake of something that might never turn out according to your dreams? Yeah, be smart and stop when it stops being fun!

Warning: If you're really dedicated, if you're passionate about your writing -- let me emphasize, passionate about **writing**, about fleshing out the stories in your head and giving faces and life to the voices in your head, writing as opposed to selling -- it gets under your skin. You can't NOT write. Even if nobody ever reads what you wrote, you have to write. It's your private therapy, escape hatch, and emergency pressure valve. It's your mental and emotional balance.

A while ago, I thought about that promise to stop when I wasn't having fun anymore. I was battling a truly wretched book, something I wrote years ago, that I had taken out of storage and revised drastically. The monster wasn't cooperating. I kept hitting roadblocks in the revision process, coming up with more and more problems that needed resolving. Ever have one of those days? Go on for months? On top of this, I had a contract book due at the same time.

Pressure, pressure, pressure! Self-imposed ulcers!

Ah, but the shriek of exhilaration, and the sounds of chains falling to the ground when I reached one goal, giving me permission to get to work on the next book. The joy and anticipation of getting back to the book that I really wanted to work on. Such fun. Yeah, FUN!

Even when I'm in agony, smacking my head against the wall and wondering why I keep doing this to myself, committing myself to writing stories I don't wanna work on anymore, I know it will soon be over and I can go back to having **fun**.

✓ *Do Yourself A Favor*: **Have fun.**

Write what interests you and feeds your heart and soul and

imagination. The stories burning in your heart, demanding to be told. Don't let others pressure you to tell **their** story, **their** way, **their** genre, **their** style, or only to write to the market. (The market changes even *before* the self-proclaimed experts finish announcing the newest or next big thing.) You'll slowly kill yourself and not ever realize it. Chances are good, the focus on writing what silences the song in your soul for the sake of money will show in your writing. Eventually, this affects your sales. Then you'll end up miserable and monumentally blocked because the muse or the girls in the basement or whatever you call your creative side has either abandoned you in a huff or is dead.

> ✓ *Do Yourself A Favor*: Write what feeds you while you're waiting for your big break. But don't just ***wait***. You need to be on the move. Constantly learn and experiment and network and be out there, looking for that opportunity. Sails need to be up, catching the wind of opportunity when it finally arrives, and your creative boat needs to be out on the water. Otherwise, by the time you respond to the wind or current change and get to the dock and put your boat in the water, it could be long gone, or have passed you by

So stick to it. Keep working. Focus on the drudgery and get it out of the way. The fun is waiting again, right around the corner.

THE SELLING PHASE:

Do Yourself a Favor: Tips and Quips on the Writing Life

THE UGLY TRUTH -- PROMOTION

Fact of the Writing Life: **Nobody** is going to sell your books for you until you sell them first.

That might sound like common sense, and at the same time, a lot of us say, "HUH?"

Well, yeah, we have to sell the books to an agent and then a publisher. Unless of course we go the self-pub route, which more and more people are doing.

The trick is getting the attention of readers -- and not just any readers, but the ones who want to read the kind of books we write. Not that easy. Because everybody is jumping on the bandwagon every time someone announces a new promotion outlet or trick. Blogs, Facebook, book signing tours, giveaways, raffles, auctions, Patreon, newsletters, etc.

Every time I pick up an article or book talking about promoting books, getting people to at least read the blurb and consider buying, someone says that *word of mouth* is still the best method of promotion. But how do you get people to talk about your book? Well, you have to get someone to read it, and get them to start talking, telling their friends. Which comes back to the beginning of the vicious circle: letting people know the book is there and getting their interest.

Someone once said that even bad publicity is worthwhile. Rotten reviews, the really scathing, virulent, poisonous reviews, get people interested -- they want to know why someone is so fired up against your book, perhaps even more interested than if someone was positively passionate about your book. I don't think I want to go that route, but think about it: how many best sellers out there became best sellers because some group went foaming-at-the-mouth, condemning-the-author-to-eternal-perdition violently against it?

(You want to really kill someone's career? Convince people NOT to talk about them. Make them vanish. I still don't understand why people pay big $$ to go to sports events specifically to boo someone who dissed our town. Keep the arena or stadium empty, don't put your money in their pockets. They aren't worth the effort of even despising them. *Sorry, another rant. Back to our regularly scheduled programming ...*)

The glory days of authors who can sit in their cozy writing rooms and do nothing but write are long over -- if they ever truly existed. Yes, the best thing you can do to promote your books is to write one great, compelling story after another. But a very, very close second is to let people know the book is **there**.

So begin talking about your book before it's published. Get a blog. Join groups where you can talk to readers -- but:

- ✓ *Do Yourself A Favor: Don't be obnoxious*! Don't spend all your online time talking about "my book, my book, my book," ad infinitum, ad nauseum. As soon as people realize you only joined their social media group to sell them something, they'll tune you out. Or worse, complain to the moderator or whoever has the power to toss you to the side of the Information Superhighway.

Offer them something they're interested in, something they want or need, something that entertains or makes them think, and then as a side note, mention you write this type or that type of books. Then when the book is released you can say, "Oh, by the way, my newest book is ..." And people will react like a friend just announced a baby has been born, or they got a new job -- they'll be congratulatory, and those who are really interested will come look. (*Yeah, I hear you -- easier said than done. Confession time: I'm still figuring it out. Look at it this way, though: Knowing where you're completely clueless and mostly helpless is half the battle!*)

It's hard. I hate promotion. I do the little I can figure out to do, at least. When I run regular ads and I post regularly and just get my name out there ... yeah, my sales pick up.

So let people know your book is coming. Find opportunities to show off your cover and talk about the story without being obnoxious. Establish yourself as someone who can be trusted, who has something to give, who is offering something they enjoy and maybe even want, so people will listen and give you a chance. Get yourself a website and/or blog, where you can post about your books and people can communicate with you, to ask questions, or even invite you to author events. Find people who are interested in what you write.

As for the rest ... once you figure it out, tell me?

PR, MARKETING, AND EDUCATION

Another ugly, painful, inescapable truth in the writing life.

You either prepare for it while you're writing (a smart move, but dealing with this inevitability can seriously dampen your creative joy) or you face it as you're in the production process (distracting you from things like formatting and edits and making decisions on the cover art) or you face it once the book is actually out there on the market, and in response to your shout of "Look, my new baby, isn't she PRETTY?!?!?!?" all you get is … crickets.

Honestly, you're lucky if you get crickets. That means there's something alive out there, and you're not shouting into a vacuum.

What am I talking about?

PR, Marketing, Publicity, Advertising, Self-Promotion. All ugly, dirty, pain-inducing words.

Okay, I'll admit, for some people, this is the fun part. These demented, over-enthusiastic, way-too-much-creative-energy people actually enjoy planning PR campaigns and coming up with loglines and finding creative, inexpensive ways to get their book title and cover art and blurbs out there to whet the appetites of readers around the globe.

Other people can't get up the nerves to tell their roommates or next door neighbors, "Oh, hey, um, by the way, if you've got nothing to do, y'know, I wrote this story and maybe, y'know, if it won't give you a headache or make you hurl, you might, like, maybe want to read it?"

Confession time: I *loathe* (with a passion equivalent to the Grinch's) doing marketing. I am a total incompetent. I would sell my first-born child (actually, that's what I'm trying to do, because my books **are** my children!) to have someone else handle all the selling chores for me. Problem is, you need money to get the attention and time of the really good marketing people.

Just like with bad agents, a bad PR or marketing guru, mentor, assistant/whatever is far worse for your writing career than having none at all. The really poisonous ones destroy your reputation and your future chances of selling even after you leave them, because editors and publishers and agents associate your name with theirs.

What do you do when doing it yourself is almost worse than having a lazy incompetent or embezzling liar or color-blind graphic artist doing it for you?

- ✓ *Do Yourself A Favor*: Start planning and asking questions and begging for mercy and help **while** you're writing the book.

Listen to podcasts devoted to marketing and getting your title and cover art and blurbs and other book information out there.

I listen to the Science Fiction Marketing Podcast, Publish Yourself (put out by Ingram Spark) and Indie Book Magic, along with audio recordings of sessions from the different writing conferences I attend.

Granted, I haven't had the time or funds to follow up on everything I've learned, but I have been learning. I've been coming up with ideas. I'm tentatively dipping my baby toe in the terrifying waters of marketing. The point is to keep learning, because the techniques that work today might not work next year, and people are constantly coming up with new outlets and new ways of getting attention. So keep learning. Yeah, I'm repeating myself. This is important enough to repeat until it soaks into your subconscious. Find out about new approaches and theories and practices. Find something that works for you, but don't tattoo it to yourself or otherwise permanently affix it to your mind and body, because the market and the outlets keep changing, and you need to change with them.

Exhausting, huh? Discouraging? Yeah. Do it anyway.

Get out there and learn. Ask questions. Try and try and try again -- and be prepared to make mistakes. Find someone with a lot more know-how and experience than you, and beg for their mercy and compassion and help.

Otherwise, **WHY** are you writing a book in the first place if you're too scared to try to sell it?

Granted, some people write for their own pleasure, but they're smart enough not to publish it anywhere. Not even on reading sites like Wattpad -- which, if you think about it, is a good place to get some exposure and maybe build up a following of readers. Post fan fiction there, post rough drafts, post freebies -- and get feedback. Who knows? You might generate enough interested readers that they start looking for your books in the online stores.

If you don't care about reaching readers, then everything you've been doing is pretty much a waste of time, or at least heavily narcissistic. Agreed?

So bite the bullet and get some education and try. And fail. And invest in lots of your favorite over-the-counter pain-reliever. Mine cycles between dark chocolate, Zero bars, and ice cream. Oh, yeah, and Tim Tams. They ain't lying when they say "Irresistible chocolaty happiness."

When you're out there trying to find people to help you, either mentoring or doing the legwork and brainwork, keep one thing in mind:

TANSTAAFL

It's taken from Heinlein, if I remember correctly: There Ain't No Such Thing As A Free Lunch.

Meaning one way or another, you're gonna have to **pay** for what you get. You have to invest, all the way down the line. Educate yourself so you can write the best book possible. Spend lots of time learning and writing. Spend lots of creative energy coming up with marketing -- and spend money on that marketing as well.

If anyone offers you something for free, when it comes to writing or publishing or marketing, I don't want to be a total cynic, but for heaven's sake, <u>approach with caution</u>. It could blow up on you. It could turn into a great big ugly barbed hook hidden inside that delicious bait. (As in far too many scam artists pretending to be publishing houses or agents. They aren't there to help authors; they're there to use authors as cash cows and hold their book rights and careers for ransom.)

Now that you've been warned: time to talk about the perils and pain of dealing with social media.

First rule: BE NICE.

Don't do like so many commercials on TV and radio and in magazines and online, and denigrate the competition. First, you're giving them free advertising by saying their names and reminding your audience they exist. Second, anything nasty you do and say will eventually come back to bite you. Just be nice. Like Mom always used to say: *If you can't say something nice, don't say anything at all.*

Don't burn your bridges. As I said elsewhere, the people you meet on the way up are the same people you meet on the way down. If you kick someone in the face on the climb up, you can bet they won't do anything to slow your fall or cushion the impact when you hit bottom. If you show mercy, it will be shown to you.

Social media is **forever**. What you say and do will never go away, good and bad. And you know Humans always remember the bad a lot more clearly than we remember the good.

I used to proofread for a legal publishing company, and the lawyer authors constantly warned about posting in any kind of social media or email. The Internet is forever. Once something is posted, it's impossible to delete it, because someone somewhere, even if just an archiving search engine, **will** pick up that one thing you want to vanish, and preserve it.

Bad publicity will hurt you forever, and come back to haunt you at the worst possible time.

Don't make arrogant, generalized statements like, "I don't read because there aren't any good books out there." Really? You've read every single book published this year alone? In every market and genre and language? A self-proclaimed writing teacher made that statement and I chose not to waste my $$ on her workshop. Her attitude would have blocked my learning anything worthwhile she might have said.

Don't steal other people's customers. Ever been to a book signing, where authors hope to have nice conversations with readers making their way down the long rows of tables, stopping to talk and ask questions and look at the books? There's always one author who can't wait his turn. The one who makes statements like, "Yeah, that's an okay book, but what you really want to read is mine." Or they just interrupt conversations, period, getting pushy and obnoxious and driving away the readers. If he would have waited a few minutes for the reader to move from that author to him, they both might have made a sale. Instead, he irritated and maybe even frightened people who came there to meet authors, and lost sales for both of them. Be courteous. Wait your turn. Even better: say nice things about the authors around you. That will impress the readers, who will remember both of you positively.

A good tactic to take is to offer readers something. If you want to generate some income, you gotta prime the pump, as they say. Give before you ask someone to give back to you. You can gain a few pounds and develop diabetes, going to book signings, with every writer putting out a bowl of candy to attract readers' attention. Yeah, candy is good, but a freebie with your website and book information on it is better. Something people will keep and use, like pens, notepads, nail files, lip balm. This can be expensive, but is ultimately long-lasting advertising, and healthier than all that sugar.

Practice courtesy and be kind. That means choosing your battles. Ignore statements that are patently false, even if they're vicious, and you feel like you're about to bleed from what you just read or someone repeated to you. Ignore the opinions, but when it comes to facts, stand up for yourself -- with facts. Let the idiots have their opinions. If you don't react, they might just fade away. Sometimes I'm convinced a lot of the people with nasty comments are just trying to generate a reaction from you, using you and tarnishing your reputation to give themselves some time in the spotlight. Don't fall into that trap. Put your ego in the freezer if you have to, or blindfold it, or just avoid review sites and blogs, if that's what it takes. Getting into arguments with reviewers or readers is just a bad idea all around.

I heard about an author who argued with someone who criticized her book in a blog post. Her first mistake was to be nasty in her response. I know some will say her first mistake was to respond at all. They're right. If she had just kept her mouth shut, or waited for her fans to jump to her defense, things might have turned out differently. But she had to fight back.

The original poster responded, defending herself from the nastiness. The author shot back more nastiness. Other people added their voices to the argument. The author kept fighting back, and got personal. More people responded. The story I heard said the blog crashed from the traffic it generated. I don't know how the war ended, but that author ultimately trashed her reputation. Not only did she lose lots of potential readers or formerly loyal fans, but agents and publishers had to have heard about it. I can just see this author walking into an appointment to pitch to an editor or agent, who decides, *Nope, no chance, I am not going to inflict this egotistical twit on my agency/publishing house.*

- ✓ *Do Yourself A Favor*: be nice! No matter how wrong and nasty your detractors are, either ignore them or thank them for their input (even if you didn't ask for it). Nothing worse for a saboteur than to get no reaction from the people they're attacking, y'know?

The Internet is forever. Remind yourself that whatever you say and do *will* eventually come back to haunt you, and always at the worst possible time. So don't say anything you don't want to hear about yourself five, ten, twenty years from now.

Unless you have a time machine and can go around preventing your bad history?

An ounce of prevention, though, takes a lot less time, and you don't have to worry about meeting yourself coming or going. Know what I mean?

Michelle L. Levigne

EDITORS AND AGENTS

Okay, your book is done -- at least, you think it's done.

Kind of hard to resist the temptation to just upload your manuscript to some online site that promises to publish your book either for very little down, or free.

Yeah, some of them are legitimate, and don't make a grab for your rights and try to tie you up for life -- and the lives and literary products of your children and grandchildren. Just because a certain crooked publisher has faded into the sunset, and tales of evil deeds seem exaggerated (sending fake police officers and lawyers after writers who dared to talk about how they were mistreated), that doesn't mean writers shouldn't be afraid of a great deal.

Where does optimism turn into gullibility? Where does caution turn into paranoia?

- ✓ *Do Yourself A Favor*: Just use common sense. Listen to your gut. Count to ten before jumping at anything that sounds incredible, out-of-this-world, or just perfect for your book. Whether it's an editor/publishing house or an agent or an indie publishing opportunity.

Do your research. Do your homework. Common sense! Make a list of the good and bad of each possibility and compare to see if you'll be better off or worse off if you say yes or no.

Someone once told me that any time someone puts pressure on you to make a decision right now, hurry, time is running out, run away! Yeah, chances are good they're pressuring you so you don't look too closely, so you don't take the time to examine things and notice there's a little old man hiding behind a curtain, pulling levers and running all sorts of special effects. If someone puts a time pressure move on you, that's a good enough warning sign to say no, thanks, maybe next time.

Take time to think and research and consider and comparison shop. Your options: Going for the golden ring of traditional publishing (including a nice little advance, emphasis on *little*); Taking a chance on a new small press (they're springing up like weeds, just make sure you're not allergic, okay?); Taking the plunge by indie publishing (doubly so, your success is totally in your hands, meaning all that marketing and promotion); Begging/blackmailing an agent to take you on as a client.

Bottom line: think and take your time.

Repeat after me: Common Sense.

I'm not going to go into whether traditional publishing is best, or indie publishing is best, or small press is best. Because I don't know!

Seriously, I've been with small press. And I'm kinda doing indie publishing now, running Mt. Zion Ridge Press. And yes, I'm still going after the big brass ring (and hoping for gold) with traditional publishing and trying to get that dream publisher to fall in love with my books.

What have I said multiple times already? *You choose what works for you -- what suits your needs -- what suits your tastes.*

More important: You choose what you *know you can handle.* The further away from traditional publishing you move, the more responsibility for your success falls on **you**. The more time and money and creative energy you have to spend on getting the attention of your audience and persuading them to give you a chance.

Okay, with that taken care of, here are a few things to think about:

Publishers:

Do your homework. Go to the publishers' websites and read what they say about themselves. Read their wish list of books they are looking for. Read their instructions for how to get your book into their hands. For goodness' sake, do not send an arrogant letter to them, along the lines of, "Yeah, I know you said you wanted A, but if you give my book a chance, you'll change your mind and love B."

After that, find out **who** you should send the book to. Translation: use names, not titles. Nothing says "random arrows" and a submission blitz than a "Dear Editor" or "Dear Fantasy Editor" or "To Whom It May Concern" cover letter.

Now here's the painful part. Especially if you've done all the work in the previous paragraph:

(Maybe you should move this step to the top of the list, before you read what the publisher says.) *Check out what their authors say about them.* Look for the complaint boards online. Look for author forums. Check out places like Preditors and Editors. http://pred-ed.com/

Or the Writer Beware page at SFWA: https://www.sfwa.org/other-resources/for-authors/writer-beware/

Then, if you hear negative things, investigate the people who are making the complaints. The ugly truth is, there are some mega-zilla prima donnas out there. People who didn't get the star treatment they thought they deserved, and they opened their nasty mouths and spilled a lot of poison, and even though there is *some* truth mixed in there, they magnified it.

What's really sad is that some of the "gripe" boards online have the attitudes that authors are *always* victims, so they don't bother investigating the complaints, or even ask for the publisher's side of the gripe. Many good publishers have been maligned unfairly, along with the authors who stood up for them.

The complainers had what they *thought* was a legitimate complaint with their publisher. Instead of going to their publisher or agent to fix the problem, they took it to the Internet, where it was blown all out of proportion. (Hint: don't expect people who have no access to facts, or the authority or influence to fix the problem, to do anything useful.) A simple, even silly misunderstanding turned into a mess. The whiners/troublemakers who didn't communicate with the people who could actually FIX the problem ended up losing their agent or their publishing contract.

For instance, one of my small publishers had offered a contract to a writer who was new to them. Shortly after she signed the contract, they learned she had posted on a couple author bulletin boards the details of her contract that irritated her. She never told them she had a problem with the clauses. In fact, she had misinterpreted the clauses. If she had just asked them for clarification, or told them she didn't like the clause, they could have worked with her. The damage was done. She had badmouthed them and didn't give them a chance to fix the problem before it went public. So they canceled the contract. They were smart enough not to trawl the Internet, watching for her to continue griping and warping the story to make herself the victim. If she was smart (doubtful) she wouldn't complain about losing the contract she wasn't happy about in the first place, because that would make her look like she couldn't make up her mind.

So, take every negative comment -- and every deliriously happy report -- with a couple grains of salt. Maybe the whole shaker.

Preparing your sales pitch:

Even if you're self-publishing, you need the same information you'd use to sell the book to an editor or agent, to sell it to your readers. Make sense?

Preparing your blurbs and elevator pitches and synopses and one-sheets is a good test of just how well you know your book. Can you condense an 80,000-word book into a 400-word back cover blurb, or an elevator pitch? I highly recommend having the book written before you write the dreaded synopsis. If you're indie publishing, you need to have blurbs of different sizes ready for all those fields to fill in when you provide the upload information for the ISBN, for the printer, the online venue, and when you're applying to get your book accepted for book fairs and craft fairs and any other event that will let you come in and hand-sell your books.

Remember to do all of these in present tense. I don't know why, but wiser heads say that present tense is more immediate and powerful.

Variously called the logline or slug line or elevator pitch: Encapsulate your book in twenty-five words, with the hero/heroine, their goal, and the challenge or obstacle to reaching that goal. It's called an elevator pitch because you have to be able to get the information out in the time it takes an elevator car to go from one floor to another.

Here's the slug line I used to query my fairy tale novel, **Bitter Sweet**:

Princess Wronged seeks justice against Prince Not-So-Charming, and learns revenge is a dish best served ... not cold, but by someone else.

Then there's the small blurb: 100 to 150 words. A little more detail. Use the log line as a foundation.

Then the back cover blurb: essentially, what you'd see on the back of a book that convinces the shopper to open up the book and read the first page, maybe flip through and read the first pages of several different chapters.

The synopsis (length varies depending on the publisher's requirements.):

- ✓ *Do Yourself A Favor*: Find out how many pages of synopsis they want, and clarify if it's single or double-spaced. That makes a big difference!)

Relate the important plot details, the steps to get from the "ordinary world" to the "return." (Check out Campbell's list of the **Hero's Journey**, or Chris Vogler's **The Artist's Journey**, for those important steps, both in writing your book and writing the dreaded, horrible, blood's-leaking-out-my-ears-from-the-agony synopsis.) Yes, there are going to be some scenes and sub-plot elements that are important to you, but if they aren't absolutely necessary to selling the story and moving the plot along, don't waste your page/word limit.

To repeat myself (warned you!), **Get Fresh Eyes**: ask people you trust, who have some writing talent, to read through the synopsis and tell you where they're confused, where there seems to be holes in the story, to help you make it right. Get help to write a synopsis that will make the editor or agent say, "Send it!"

One-sheet. What's a one-sheet? Well ... one sheet of paper, one side of that paper. A little bit of decoration, some color, a graphic, something that "fits" the mood or genre or theme of the story. Give the title, the genre, the word count. Then write an overview statement of the whole book, or series, if you're trying to pitch the first book of a series. Keep it short and simple. A logline or elevator pitch is good. Then, a condensed synopsis (after all this practice, you should have this nailed -- or close to it). Don't treat it like a back cover blurb, because the blurb is to induce people to pick up the book and read, and you don't want to give away any spoilers, right? With this one-sheet, you're convincing the editor or agent to give you a chance to send sample chapters and synopsis, or the whole book, for consideration. So don't make the ending or resolution a mystery. Spoilers encouraged.

This is a one-sheet I did that my agent liked -- still waiting to sell. (Anyone? Anyone?)

Magic to Spare
Fantasy/Humor -- 107,550 words
"Fractured Fairy Tales" starring Scarlet O'Hara

Book 1 of 3: The Kindness Curse

Young Queen Merrigan is cursed, trapped in an old body, wandering foreign kingdoms. Granted, her recently deceased husband was a selfish idiot, and maybe he *was* a little wicked, but why should *she* suffer for his crimes?

The "injustice" she suffers motivates her to (grudgingly) get involved with the downtrodden and innocent. She supports herself by sewing, and while working in a corrupt judge's household, she repairs a magical book named Bib. He becomes her advisor and companion.

They befriend a mermaid, hunting for the knife a cruel prince used to cut off her hair, so she can regain her tail and return to the sea. Next is a princess under a stupidity curse. They meet a merchant in search of the most beautiful cloth in the world, and stumble into an "Emperor's New Clothes" situation. Working in a warehouse full of orphans, they befriend Belinda, a fugitive princess hunted by unworthy princes and betrayed by pea soup.

Belinda's true love, Bayl, tracks her down. With him is his brother Bryan, Merrigan's childhood sweetheart. Bryan doesn't recognize her as an old woman, and they become friends all over again. When Belinda's evil sisters come to destroy her happily-ever-after, Merrigan takes their enchanted apple, and bites it. She could use some peace and quiet, after months dealing with a warehouse full of children.

Sacrificing herself for Belinda breaks the curse on Merrigan, that she will wander in disguise until she learns to care for others. Bryan recognizes her, kisses her, and awakens her.

In Book 2, ***Maven of Magic***, Merrigan and Bryan journey to her father's kingdom, and unravel a plot to ration all magic in the world. They discover that Nanny Tulip, who turned Merrigan into a spoiled brat, is involved.

Book 3, ***Magic and Thorns***, looks backward to Merrigan's childhood (in the vein of Marissa Meyers' ***Fairest***) and how Nanny Tulip turned her into a brat, intending to use her to destroy all happily-ever-afters.

After you do this, you need to leave some space for your biography (training, writing credits, awards, your agent if you have one, and contact information for both of you) , and a head-shot.
Easy, huh?
(Hah!)
Now, here's something that's kind of obvious, but the funny thing about writers is that we sometimes gloss over the obvious. That's why we need friends, why we need to ask for help, why we need to get fresh eyes to look over our work after we've gone over our stories so many times that they're written on our corneas -- all ten drafts.

Get fresh eyes to look over your proposals and cover letters and back cover blurbs and synopses **before** you send them to the publicist or editor or agent or contest or wherever they're going to end up. Ask for input and feedback.

Then here's the part that isn't so obvious: Take responsibility for your book or proposal or query letter or whatever. If there's a glitch after all that work, don't you dare blame your beta readers or critique group or whoever.

YOU are responsible for whatever goes out there. *Sorry if I've killed your fallback plan of blaming somebody else for your mistakes (Hey, if it didn't work for Adam ...)*

Another obvious-thing-some-people-never-think-of:
Be nice to the editors or agents or whoever you're dealing with.
Yeah, that *shouldn't* have to be said but admit it, while writers are mostly introverts, we're kind of arrogant too. Am I right?

Learn the rules, follow the rules, never, ever, on pain of death expect to be given an exception.

But that doesn't mean you can't ask.
That's the operative word.
Ask!!!
Never demand.
Never whine.

Never connive.

Ask.

Begging and bribery are time-honored tactics -- just don't be obnoxious or try to guilt-trip people into giving you an exception to the rules. Find out if there's anything that will soften up or surprise your desired agent or editor or mentor or critique leader.

The operative word is to ASK. What's the worst that could happen? If you get a "no," at least you've had practice for asking. And asking again. Until you get that yes. An answer of any kind is better than no answer whatsoever because you didn't ask.

Just be courteous, okay?

Then (do I need to tell you this?), when you do get the contract, whether it's with a publisher or agent, be ready to swallow your pride yet again ... and again. Be flexible. Do what you're asked to do, and try to always get it done ahead of schedule. If you promise you'll get something back to them in two weeks, do it in twelve days. Always amaze by over-delivering. Do what your publisher or editor asks -- and don't make them remind you or ask a second or third time. This is one of those times when you need to be the yes-man and apple-polisher.

When you get your galleys, for heaven's sake, don't check out the font and the arrangement of the words on the page, to make sure it's pretty, and then ignore the actual words on the page. In these days of the world being run by computers, it's entirely possible someone somewhere will press the wrong button and something will be messed up with your book, just before it goes to print. Such as entire pages going missing, and chapters repeating, or the wrong version of the book being typeset. It happens!

I repeat: No matter how many people have had their hands on your book, **<u>you are the ultimate and last authority</u>** and final person responsible for what goes onto the pages and is bound and wrapped in a cover and sent to the stores. So know your book and go over your galley proofs and look at the words. Make sure all the words are there, and they're in the right order. Being "pretty" won't do you any good if the wrong words are there.

And don't whine when you're not at the top of their list. You're the new kid. You're at the bottom of the totem pole, the bottom of the pyramid, whatever. Until you're on the NY Times bestseller list and you have several multi-book contracts under your belt, consider yourself undeserving of your editor's or agent's time and attention. It'll help stop the whining and wondering if your agent needs to check her Rolodex to remember your name.

And always remember to ask.

Do Yourself a Favor: Tips and Quips on the Writing Life

THE QUEST FOR COVER ART

Ah, cover art. (Or sometimes, aarrgghh! Cover art!)

Love it or hate it (sometimes those are the only two choices you have, two extremes) cover art is a vital element in the sales of your books. The horror of cover art is that sometimes you have absolutely no input, no control, no voice, no influence in what gets put on your book.

There's the (probably apocryphal, changed every time it's told) story of a book where the cover showed an Amazon with long black hair. The back cover blurb described her as a petite nymph with short red curls. The heroine as described by the writer (whose text was not consulted in creating an element to <u>help sell the book</u>) was of medium build with long, white-blonde hair.

Go figure.

Chances are good, if the author got to see the cover art before it was finalized, and was allowed to have any input whatsoever, and protested the inaccuracies and inconsistencies, the response from the art department would be (choose one):

"It's set in stone, too late to change now."

"We paid too much money for this, the budget doesn't allow for re-dos."

"We like this better -- can you change your book to suit it?"

Then there is the story of a "name" writer in romance whose cover art came out with **three** arms on the heroine. The publisher caught this glitch after the books had been shipped, and tried to get the books back to be destroyed, making the limited books in existence collector's items. The author was smart enough to capitalize on it and build up a buzz for her book in the process.

My own horror story is what I call my "stripper Zorro" cover. I described the heroine as being a "daughter of Zorro" type, dressed head to foot in black, with a cape and floppy-brimmed hat, sitting astride a black beast that was a cross between a bat and a horse, looking down on the hero in space-age body armor. What the publisher gave me was some bimbo in a seductive pose, shown from shoulders to calves, dressed in a black patent leather bikini, a glossy wet suit-type jacket, and thigh-high black boots. When I complained, the publisher said, "Sex sells." The problem was that there was only **one kiss** in the entire story, and it was a "Thanks for saving my life" kiss (about the same heat level between Leia and Luke before they swung across the gap inside the Death Star). Problem: when you promise something with the cover art and the book doesn't deliver, that makes readers **angry**.

Gee, I have no idea why ...

Then you get publishers who make up for all the pain by making you participate in creating the cover. True, the fifteen-page questionnaire is another type of pain, but it's **worth it**.

- ✓ *Do Yourself A Favor*: Do **not** complain when you get a chance to have input on your cover art (even when the process twists your brain into knots). If you did your prep work, clearly describing your characters' appearance, if you know your story well enough to know the theme and key moments and you plan ahead for the cover art, to know your ideal cover scene, how hard can it be? You might not get what you want, your *ideal* cover, but your input helps ensure the cover art **fits the story**. Or at least is more appropriate than a fantasy cover with unicorns and mermaids, when the story is a hard science fiction techno-thriller set inside an asteroid during a power outage!

The point of all this? Everyone judges a book by its cover. When you can, work with your publisher to make sure the judgment is the right one, and the cover gives a good idea of what readers will find inside. The effort is well worth it. Be prepared to fill out that questionnaire. Be ready to answer questions about the elements and images vital to the story, and the "feeling" you want to convey with the cover art. This is your baby -- be involved as much as you can. Push to be involved more than they want to allow you.

IN CONCLUSION

- ✓ So ***Do Yourself A Favor*** and learn what's hard-and-fast, and what is flexible. It'll save you pain and effort and wasted time in the long run.

You only have so much time, so much energy, so much creativity and so much money for promotion, so choose carefully before you commit and spend

Michelle L. Levigne

About the Author

On the road to publication, Michelle fell into fandom in college and has 40+ stories in various SF and fantasy universes. She has a bunch of useless degrees in theater/English/film/communication/writing. Even worse, she has (or had) nearly 100 books and novellas with multiple small presses, in science fiction and fantasy, YA, and sub-genres of romance.

Her official launch into publishing came with winning first place in the Writers of the Future contest in 1990. She was a finalist in the EPIC Awards competition multiple times, winning with *Lorien* in 2006 and *The Meruk Episodes, I-V,* in 2010, and was a finalist in the 2018 Realm Award competition, in conjunction with the Realm Makers convention.

Her training includes the Institute for Children's Literature; proofreading at an advertising agency; and working at a community newspaper. She is a tea snob and freelance edits for a living (MichelleLevigne@gmail.com for info/rates), but only enough to give her time to write. Her newest crime against the literary world is to be co-managing editor at Mt. Zion Ridge Press. Be afraid … be very afraid.

www.Mlevigne.com
www.MichelleLevigne.blogspot.com
@MichelleLevigne

www.ingramcontent.com/pod-product-compliance
Lightning Source LLC
Chambersburg PA
CBHW031156020426
42333CB00013B/696